CW00522023

Milton's
Words

Milton's Words

ANNABEL PATTERSON

OXFORD
UNIVERSITY PRESS

Great Clarendon Street, Oxford OX2 6DP

Oxford University Press is a department of the University of Oxford.
It furthers the University's objective of excellence in research, scholarship,
and education by publishing worldwide in

Oxford New York

Auckland Cape Town Dar es Salaam Hong Kong Karachi
Kuala Lumpur Madrid Melbourne Mexico City Nairobi
New Delhi Shanghai Taipei Toronto

With offices in

Argentina Austria Brazil Chile Czech Republic France Greece
Guatemala Hungary Italy Japan Poland Portugal Singapore
South Korea Switzerland Thailand Turkey Ukraine Vietnam

Oxford is a registered trade mark of Oxford University Press
in the UK and in certain other countries

Published in the United States
by Oxford University Press Inc., New York

British Library Cataloguing in Publication Data

Data available

Library of Congress Cataloging in Publication Data

Library of Congress Control Number: 2009931632

Typeset by SPI Publisher Services, Pondicherry, India
Printed in Great Britain
on acid-free paper by
Clays Ltd., St Ives plc

ISBN 978-0-19-957346-2

1 3 5 7 9 10 8 6 4 2

ACKNOWLEDGMENTS

Many years ago, it was reported to me that Arthur Barker wished I would write a book on Milton. He was, is, one of the many Miltonists, dead and alive, who made me feel that I was somehow under contract to do just that; several essays, articles, and chapters on Milton notwithstanding, I still had not tackled the most demanding topic, passed the most rigorous test, that literary studies in the early modern period offers. 'Yet ease and leasure', I can imagine Barker saying reproachfully, 'was given thee for thy retired thoughts out of the sweat of other persons.' That ease and leisure was never more demanding than during the last two years, during which I was the recipient of an Emeritus Fellowship from the Mellon Foundation, a brilliant device to keep retirees at their desks. First, I wrote *The Long Parliament of Charles II*, which continued my lifelong interest in Milton's friend Andrew Marvell. Then I was supposed to be working on a book on representations of democracy in American culture, when I suddenly got waylaid by the idea of a little book that would draw on some of my previous Milton work, revised and expanded, but tie everything together under the concept of 'Milton's Words', an old-fashioned omnibus that we need to see back on the road. So my first thanks are to the Mellon Foundation and the Yale Koerner Center for Emeritus Faculty, where I sit in a gracious office surrounded by my Milton library, a privilege that many retirees miss. In this arena I am particularly grateful to the help, practical, social, and psychological, that Bernard Lytton, Alan Trachtenberg, Patricia Dallai, and Margaret Hionis provide at the Koerner Center.

It would be quite impossible to specify the personal and professional riches that I have inherited or extracted from the world of Milton scholars on both sides of the Atlantic. I must start with David Quint and Nigel Smith, who generously read the whole manuscript and claimed to enjoy it, John Rogers and Dayton Haskin, who helped me out with *Paradise Regained*, and Martin Dzelzainis, who did the same with *The Readie and Easie Way*. It turns out, when I look back on my life, that nine-tenths of my closest friends are Miltonists, and every time I meet up with them again I am enlightened, occasionally chastened, but always re-energized. Joseph Wittreich is perhaps my oldest Miltonist friend, providing years of encouragement, and I am particularly grateful to him for writing *Why Milton Matters*. Stanley Fish and I have been affectionate competitors for ever, it seems. Albert Labriola has shepherded the Milton Society of America with wit and fairness for so long that he has become an allegorical personage. If I start listing all the others I might lose a friend whose name went somehow missing. So I'll stop here, and just thank you all. You know who you are.

A.P., 2009

CONTENTS

ABBREVIATIONS USED IN THE TEXT

CE	F. A. Patterson et al. (eds.), *The Works of John Milton*, 18 vols. in 21, New York, 1931–8. Columbia Edition.
CPW	Don M. Wolfe et al. (eds.). *Complete Prose Works of John Milton*, 8 vols. New Haven, 1953–82
PL	*Paradise Lost*
PR	*Paradise Regained*
RCG	*Reason of Church Government*
REW	*Readie & Easie Way*

Introduction

In 1963 Oxford University Press published a short book with a large title: *Milton's Grand Style*. Its author was Christopher Ricks, who at the then prodigious age of 30 took on two of the great arbiters of English literary criticism and taste, F. R. Leavis and T. S. Eliot, who in tandem established the reign of Modernism. Neither Leavis nor Eliot approved of the way Milton wrote poetry. They did not care a jot about his work in prose, despite the fact that it was the source of his fame in his lifetime, the admiration of eighteenth-century Whigs, and the inspiration of several of the Founding Fathers of America. Instead Leavis and Eliot had inherited from eighteenth-century editors and critics, most notably Dr. Johnson and Richard Bentley, the belief that poetry should be judged, word by word, phrase by phrase, according to current tastes. Both Johnson and Bentley, for different reasons, judged that Milton's poetry was florid, unnatural to the ear, over-Latinate, and generally over-written. Leavis and Eliot fastened on the idea of unnaturalness (as if poetry were ever a natural way to communicate), and with Shakespeare and John Donne as their standards from the past, wrote new laws. In Milton's poetry, Eliot declared in his British Academy lecture of 1947:

There is always the maximal, never the minimal, alteration of ordinary language. Every distortion of construction, the foreign idiom, the use of a word in a foreign way or with the meaning of the foreign word from which it is derived rather than the accepted meaning in English, every idiosyncrasy is a particular act of violence which Milton has been the first to commit. There is no cliché, no poetic diction in the derogatory sense, but a perpetual sequence of original acts of lawlessness.

The Academy Lecture was supposed to be a softening of Eliot's original position, as laid down in *Essays and Studies* in 1936, that Milton was just a bad writer, but it was an apology that left the main reason for disapproval untouched. 'A perpetual sequence of original acts of *lawlessness*', according to a penal code not in existence when Milton wrote! As for Leavis, in 1947 he published *Revaluation*, including an essay on 'Milton's Verse' that celebrated Eliot's 'dislodgement' of Milton from the English literary pantheon. In 'cultivating so complete and systematic a callousness to the intrinsic nature of English, Milton forfeits all possibility of subtle or delicate life in his verse'. Milton deserved what he got—demotion.

Christopher Ricks turned this evaluative principle upside down. In his clever hands, the Grand Style proved itself endlessly capable of yielding small gems and subtle effects. Ricks's book changed the way critics and teachers could evaluate Milton's style, but its argument remained within the frame of taste, of approval or disapproval, already established. Its point was that Leavis and Eliot were not good enough readers to see, if one had not decided against it in advance, how constantly *interesting* Milton's style actually was. *Milton's Grand Style* was followed, in 1990, by Thomas Corns's *Milton's Language*, which adopted the Ricksian position but backed it up with stylistics, which substitutes for the special and fascinating instance a generalizing impulse, supported where possible by computer-derived statistics. And in 1997 Corns was followed by John Hale's *Milton's Languages*, the first book to deal thoroughly with the fact, and the consequences of the fact, that Milton was multi-lingual, and wrote as much in Latin as in English. Hale countered the charge that Milton's style was over-Latinate by applying Ricks's methods to some of Milton's most Latinate words and constructions, to happy effect.

As the titles above reveal, 'style' is just another word for 'language', and 'language', of course, means primarily *words*, the choice of words and their arrangement in units of sense and communication. But because of the apologetic or defensive structure of pro-Milton criticism in the later twentieth and early twenty-first century, sense and communication as the goal of word-use in poetry have been largely ignored in favor of 'effect'. Now, about half a century after Leavis wrote the 'stern letter' that provoked Ricks to his brilliant and salutary reply, we are free to admire Milton again; but, oddly, the positive reassessments we now take for granted have not much advanced our understanding of *how* and *why* Milton used words in the extraordinary ways (for there were many) that he did. To some extent, this kind of inquiry *has* been initiated in the study of Milton's prose works, increasingly the center of attention since Milton studies became explicitly (as distinct from secretly, as in

Johnson and Eliot) a site of struggle between different political persuasions. But nobody, to my knowledge, has attempted to chart, analyze, and understand Milton's use of words, in both the poetry and prose, as the product of a single mind and a writing life; still less as a product that changed in response to different circumstances.

A couple of salient examples may help explain what needs to be done.

UNLIBIDINOUS. Suppose we take Milton's editorial comment on his statement that while Adam and the archangel Raphael ate the food she had prepared, 'Meanwhile at Table | Eve ministered naked ... | ... but in those hearts | Love unlibidinous reign'd' (*PL* 5: 443–49). 'Unlibidinous' is clearly one of those words to which Leavis and Eliot should have objected, both on the grounds of its Latin origin and on its 'unnatural' placement between 'Love' and 'reign'd', whereas normal English would say either 'in those hearts unlibidinous Love reign'd', or, less likely, 'in those hearts Love reign'd unlibidinous'. To which Ricks would have replied that the word's euphonious central placement, the 'syntactical fluidity' thereby created (p. 138) allows it to refer in meaning in both directions, thus making the statement worthy of more careful attention. At this point in the conversation, Corns (pp. 85–86) identifies it both as Milton's coinage (whereas 'libidinous' was well established) and as one of a series of negative compounds beginning with 'un' of which Milton is particularly fond, and which can also be found in the prose. Corns does not, however, exert his own stylistic principles to document just how fond, numerically, or draw any conclusions from the observation. In 'Negativity' I show that Milton's attraction to such negative positives is characteristic of his style from the beginning, and that it has its origins both in his Latin training and in his agonistic image of himself as a writer. In this particular instance, 'unlibidinous' answers his complaint in the autobiographical section of *Reason of Church Government* (1641) about the 'writings and interludes of libidinous and ignorant Poetasters' who are corrupting their Stuart audiences and whom he hopes one day in the future to shame and replace with himself (*CPW* 1: 818). Between the two words and eras lie the vast tracts of his writings in favor of divorce on the basis of incompatibility, in which Milton wrestled with the vocabulary of the libido and the carnality of canon law; and (to use quite a different critical approach) the rampant libidinousness of the court of Charles II, to which 'unlibidinous' may compare itself in a non-syntactical form of reference. Finally there is Milton's peculiar introduction of divorce and polygamy as a topic into his Latin treatise *De Doctrina Christiana*, where a Hebrew king, Joash, 'was induced to take two wives, not by licentious passion (*non regia libido*), but by the advice of a wise and holy priest' (*CE* 15: 150). This is what Ricks would have called 'cross-reference' in Milton's works, but he only traces it in the poetry, and only in terms of patterns of imagery. That certain words, already dense with meaning, could perform acts of cross-reference to themselves, could argue with each other, was not part of his remit.

I N D E F A T I G A B L E . Six syllables long, 'indefatigable' is clearly a Latin adjective, found in Seneca (*De Ira*, 2.12.7). As an adjective it had been transported into English by Robert Burton, in the *Anatomy of Melancholy*, which we know Milton read. As an adverb, it had been adopted much earlier by William Webbe, in his *Discourse of English Poetry* (1586), in a context that would have interested Milton:

> Master Arthur Golding, which ... traveleth as yet indefatigably, and is addicted without society by his continuall laboure, to profit this nation and speech in all kind of good learning.   (ciii^r)

The word was often used in the context of reading or scholarly endeavor. Milton himself adopted it to his praise of the Long Parliament in the exordium to *Areopagitica* (*CPW* 2: 487), where their 'laudable deeds' and 'indefatigable vertues' in bringing the second English Reformation so far are mentioned as the basis and motive for now recalling a noxious piece of legislation, the Licensing Act of 1643. *Areopagitica* was, of course, a tract that used heroic language in favor of scholarly freedom. We know that Andrew Marvell read it, and can assume he had done so by 1650, when he took it adverbially to motivate Oliver Cromwell to more military victories at the end of the *Horatian Ode*:

> But thou the Wars and Fortunes Son
> March indefatigably on.

And Marvell was quoting himself when in 1654, in the *First Anniversary of the Government under O.C.*, he contrasted Cromwell to the 'heavy' and unproductive kings of Europe who 'neither build the Temple in their days | Nor Matter for succeeding

Founders raise'. Meanwhile 'indefatigable Cromwell hyes, | And cuts his way still nearer to the Skyes' (ll. 45–46). Marvell had achieved the seemingly impossible task of bending an uneuphonious six-syllabled word, a mouthful, to iambic verse.

It is possible that by now 'indefatigable' (unwearied, incapable of being tired) will once more need a gloss in student editions. It is not a word to which Milton's editors have paid any special attention when it appears in *Paradise Lost*, Book 2, in Satan's phony description of his intended assault on Eden as a heroic enterprise for which a special candidate (himself) is required:

> Who shall tempt with wandring feet
> The dark unbottom'd infinite Abyss
> And through the palpable obscure find out
> His uncouth way, or spread his aery flight
> Upborne with indefatigable wings
> Over the vast abrupt.   (ll. 404–09)

You can see that Milton has learned from Marvell the art of fitting that 'uncouth' word smoothly into verse. You can see that here the first two un-words are not positives disguised as negatives but actual negatives, scary with the ideas of free fall and unknown territory. You might infer, therefore, and especially because it is Satan speaking, speaking speciously, that 'indefatigable' is here also not a positive disguised by syntax as a negative, but a negative doubly darkened by its context. So what does it say to Marvell's second Cromwellian 'indefatigable', which also imagines a flying superhuman figure? I cannot believe that these astonishing words, used only twice by Milton, are not cross-references to each other and Marvell's, implying that Satan is the dark shadow of Marvell's heroic Cromwell. We know that by 1667, when he published *Paradise Lost*, Milton no longer shared his friend's admiration for Cromwell; he had also, by the way, demolished his own image of a heroic Long Parliament.

But it would be misleading only to focus on the kind of learned or invented polysyllabic words to which Leavis and Eliot objected. Milton could, when he thought it appropriate, use plain 'native' words better than anyone. His *Ode on the Morning of Christ's Nativity* uses the little word 'no' multiple times to powerful effect, not least in its rebuke to premature optimism: 'But wisest Fate says No, | This must not yet be so'. And one of its most memorable lines defines this moment of world peace as that time when 'Birds of Calm sit brooding on the charmed wave'. 'Birds', 'sit', 'brooding', and 'wave' (from 'waw') are all Anglo-Saxon, 'calm' and 'charm' were naturalized from middle French in the fourteenth century. Note that Milton does *not* use the learned but then fashionable word 'halcyon', a favorite with the Caroline poets. Milton is far more likely to use predominantly 'native' words, especially monosyllables, when writing in rhyme, in order to exploit the 'natural' force of the plain, the common, but common because vital word, when in rhyming position; or, to reverse this point, far more likely to use learned, polysyllabic words when reinventing blank verse, which of course he learned from Shakespeare. One has only to compare his 1634 *Maske at Ludlow*, his first experiment with blank verse, with his subtly rhymed 1637 elegy, *Lycidas*, to see this distinction in early action.

This little book begins the long project of seeing what Milton's words look like when we acknowledge their freight of personal and political history; when we track them from text to text; when we consider not only the big, important, learned words but also the very small ones, such as 'perhaps', which Milton deployed with consummate skill at some crucial moments in both poetry and prose, or the phrase 'he who', which replicates the Latinate 'ille qui', but to which Milton gives a psychological twist; when we consider not only word frequency, but infrequency, uniqueness or near uniqueness, as a signal of Milton's interest in a word; when we tackle these issues in the Latin texts for which there is not, as yet, a concordance; when we consider the possibility that certain words gain or lose value for Milton as he proceeds through his writer's life, and that certain words become keywords to a particular text, as 'book' becomes to *Areopagitica*; when we reconsider the question of Milton's coinages not from the stern legalistic perspective as to whether he should have made them, but why he needed them. No one person could complete all these tasks, and nobody would wish to read a book that appeared to have completed them. Understanding Milton's words is, and should remain, a work in progress.

But close attention to Milton's words is not all that this book offers. It tells a slightly different story about Milton himself than the ones we have been used to. Starting with an abbreviated *Life*, it explains the shape of Milton's writing career, the life-long tension between his literary ambitions and the pressure of exhilarating political circumstances. The Milton you will find here walked no straight path from his Cambridge degree to the epic he had been talking of writing when he was still at university, but instead cut his teeth as a writer in an entirely different field, political controversy. The effect on his vocabulary of his campaign to reform his country's church government and its divorce laws was galvanic, not least because he had to reconstitute his own image from that of a shy and bookish person to that of a crusader. He discovered that he enjoyed not only verbal conflict, but also mudslinging, and rude words became part of his arsenal in his very first prose tract. 'Marriage' and 'divorce', on the other hand, became loaded words for Milton for personal reasons, and he developed a new set of verbal resources, which I call 'words of avoidance', to help him tackle the subject. He never got over the experience of writing the divorce tracts. It was still on his mind when at the end of his life he revised his Latin treatise on theology, *De Doctrina Christiana*.

Then, for about a decade, he was called upon to justify the Long Parliament's execution of Charles I, which forced him to come to terms with the political keywords of his generation, words such as 'king', 'liberty', 'tyranny', and 'the people'. When the republican experiment collapsed on the death of Oliver Cromwell, after one last brave salvo against the restoration of the monarchy Milton retired back into the role of private intellectual and poet. This we all know; but because the poetry and the prose have been segregated for so long, and still tend to be read as separate enterprises, we have not tended to track Milton's favorite political words into the great poems, where, as we *perhaps* unwillingly will see, they change their valence. In general, though it is impossible to do justice to all of Milton's feats of word-use and arrangement, this book will tell a complete

tale of Milton the man; his psychological trajectory as well as
that more formal notion, his 'character'; his mistakes as well
as his masterpieces.

Let me recall the wonderful description of 'Master Arthur
Golding' that, in all probability, Milton encountered in reading
William Webbe's guide to late sixteenth-century poetry: Golding
'travelleth as yet indefatigably, and is addicted without society,
by his continuall laboure, to profit this nation and speech in
all kind of good learning'. Webbe must mean 'travaileth as yet
indefatigably', and by 'without society' he must mean alone,
without colleagues. That sounds like Milton, who believed he
had a lonely mission, a calling, to educate the English, and was
more indefatigable a reader than we can imagine, demanding
similar standards from his students. In the last book of *Paradise
Regained*, however, he seems to acknowledge weariness:

> However, many *books*
> Wise men have said are wearisome; who reads
> Incessantly, and to his reading brings not
> A spirit and judgment equal or superior
> (And what he brings, what needs he elsewhere seek)
> Uncertain and unsettl'd still remains,
> Deep verst in *books* and shallow in himself,   (4: 321–27)

Framed by two dubious appearances of the word 'books', Milton's great keyword in *Areopagitica*, when he wrote at the
height of enthusiasm for books and reading, these lines are
delivered by Jesus in his notorious rejection of a life of scholarship,
the last of the kingdoms offered by Satan as bait. I take these

lines to be autobiographical not only for Milton at almost the end of his life, but also for myself, who in this short book have taken the liberty to be frugal, not to say parsimonious, with references to other scholars. Reading Ricks's deft but deferential pages, promiscuous with references to Mr. This and Dr. That, very few of whom we still recognize, it seems time for a change in procedure. Especially given the tendency of literary criticism to go out of style, Leavis and Eliot being two of the most striking instances, it is better to focus the reader's attention on Milton's words alone. The final list of works used, if not cited, is intended to partially cover this lapse of due deference; and the community of scholars from whom I have learned, for half a century, to understand Milton better, are here nonetheless, as geniuses of the shore, or guardian angels, or just good friends.

A Writing Life

At the prodigious age of 19, John Milton was chosen to address his fellow undergraduates at Cambridge at a 'Vacation Exercise', which he conducted partly in Latin, partly in English. When he came to the English section, he produced his first writer's manifesto or statement of ambition:

> Hail native Language, that by sinews weak
> Didst move my first endeavoring tongue to speak,
> And mad'st imperfect words with childish trips,
> Half unpronounc't, slide through my infant lips,
>
> .   .   .   .
>
> Here I salute thee and thy pardon ask,
> That now I use thee in my latter task;

That is, in the second part of his performance, rather than the first. The lines are almost doggerel, a presumably intentional comic self-deflation, as this is a parody of a poet's invocation of his muse. The doggerel continues:

> I have some naked thoughts that rove about
> And loudly knock to have their passage out;

> And weary of their place do only stay
> Till thou hast deck't them in thy best array.

But we can tell it is self-mockery by what follows, immediately recognizable as *our* Milton, however young:

> Yet I had rather, if I were to choose,
> Thy service in some graver subject use,
> Such as may make thee search thy coffers round,
> Before thou clothe my fancy in fit sound:
> Such where the deep transported mind may soar
> Above the wheeling poles, and at Heavn's door
> Look in...

But the young Milton had no idea how long it would take him to achieve this linguistic and imaginative goal—almost forty years—nor for how many other purposes he would search the coffers of the English language.

What follows is a very short *Life* of Milton that aims to introduce to the readers of this book, should they need such an introduction, the man who wrote the words that are our focus. There are three governing premises: first, we cannot understand Milton's use of words if we exclude from our inquiry the very large body of work he wrote in prose; second, our renewed freedom to venerate him does not require us to admire everything he wrote; and third, his life is more truly interesting if we recognize in it, rather than a coherent pattern of intentions fulfilled and principles clear from the start, a series of changes of direction, impulsive gestures, apologies, revisions, and thoughts worked out in the very process of writing them down.

Milton was born in 1608, just a few years into the reign of James I, and died about half way through the reign of Charles II, in 1674. He was apparently intended to be either a clergyman or some form of independent scholar/author, but the clerical option was soon dropped. Instead, his life was irresistibly shaped by what happened in the middle of the seventeenth century—the first English revolution against Charles I, father of Charles II, which produced first a civil war, then a republic, then a dictatorship under Oliver Cromwell, and finally came full circle with the recall of Charles II to the English throne. Milton was drawn deep into this conflict. He first became what we today would call a public intellectual, second an apologist for the revolutionary government that had just executed their king, and eventually a figure in the international press of Europe, to which he communicated in Latin.

In 1660, when Charles II returned to England, Milton was obviously in some danger for his attacks on the king's father. He was also completely blind, a condition that developed during, and was exacerbated by, his work for the revolutionary government. He survived the Restoration, after a brief spell in prison, by returning to private life, writing poetry, finishing up earlier projects like his textbooks on Ramist logic and Latin grammar, and depending heavily on readers and secretaries, including his daughters. It is amazing, however, what he was able to accomplish as a blind scholar and writer; in 1660, for example, he performed the most detailed revision of one of his pamphlets, the *Readie & Easie Way to Establish a Free Commonwealth*, possibly with the assistance of Marchamont Nedham (Worden).

And what emerged in 1667 was *Paradise Lost*, and in 1671, the year before his death, *Paradise Regained* and *Samson Agonistes*.

Paradise Lost made him a famous national poet and hence the object of critical debates such as those reviewed in my Introduction. But one cannot understand the great poems without also knowing his political views and arguments, as worked out in the heat of controversy, between 1640 and 1660. And it would be a mistake to consider him hors de combat after 1660, for there is one tract, *Of True Religion*, which in 1673 engages the fierce debates of the day about religious toleration.

From the beginning, Milton supplied his readers with accounts of his life and literary ambitions. Without actually sitting down to write his Life, he managed to insert large chunks of autobiography into other projects, to such a degree that John Diekhoff was able to publish these 'digressions' under the title of *Milton on Himself*. Their testimony as to facts needs to be taken with salt. But Milton's desire to control the record is itself one of the more interesting biographical facts about him.

At Cambridge, where his well-off scrivener father sent him to get a gentleman's education, Milton's sense of himself as designed for a great literary future was expressed in an important personal notebook, the 'Trinity Manuscript', named after the college library that preserves it, as distinct from Milton's own college, which was Christ's. In this manuscript he recorded his early poems in the order in which they were composed, sometimes noting the dates of composition or the age at which he wrote them. But in his later autobiographical digressions Milton did not specify dates, and always proffered a neater, more high-minded account of his motives than that which biographers have pieced together.

Miltonists like to see his early 'period', his excellent schooling, his time at Cambridge, his period of private study at his father's estate at Horton, and his extended tour of Italy, the social and conventional culmination of his education, as decisive in certain ways. This was the phase of 'intellectual development', as Harris Fletcher called it, thought to explain the poet he became. What Milton himself felt, however, was that he suffered from writer's block. In 1632 he complained, in Sonnet 7: 'My late spring no bud or blossom show'th | And inward ripeness doth much less appear, | That some more timely happy spirits endu'th.' In bulk, at least half of his output was in Latin, and the so-called 'prolusions' were required university essays. The form of block that he suffered was, perhaps, unrealistically large ideas of what litera-ture could be, impossible of fulfilment by a novice. In 1628 he had outlined, however vaguely, grand metaphysical or heroic subjects he hoped in future to address. But by 1642 he had still not decided what kind of great poem to write, as he admits in a long autobiographical aside in the *Reason of Church Govern-ment*, one of the earliest of the pamphlets by which his original goal had been derailed.

Nevertheless, Milton did write some successful poems before his Continental tour. In the first of these, dated 1629, he estab-lished an early claim to become a major new religious poet. This was 'On the Morning of Christ's Nativity', which goes far beyond the stable in Bethlehem to consider the eventual re-demption of the world by Christ, all folded into a brilliant prolepsis that is withdrawn as soon as it is offered: 'But wisest Fate says No, | This must not yet be so.' The next religious poem he tried, 'The Passion', collapsed after eight stanzas. It would take thirty-five years to prove his claim good.

At Cambridge Milton had also started to write sonnets, in Italian and English, a genre to which he would remain committed for the next twenty years. In 1630 he wrote, or at least dated, a sonnet-like poem in praise of Shakespeare, which had the honor of being included in the Second Folio of Shakespeare's plays when it appeared in 1632. Possibly as a result, in 1634 he received a rather important dramatic and social commission—to write a masque for the installation of John, earl of Bridgewater, as Lord President of Wales. The intermediary was Milton's friend Henry Lawes, a musician with court connections. Generically, the Masque sits uncertainly between the court masques of the day and something more intellectually and morally demanding. It was published by Lawes, though still as anonymous, in late 1637 or early 1638, and mistakenly appropriated to the canon of Milton's greatest college rival, Thomas Randolph. Finally, in 1638, not long before he left for Italy, one of his most ambitious poems was published with his name attached: *Lycidas*, an elegy for a young man he had known at Cambridge and who had drowned in a shipwreck in the Irish Channel, was included with other elegies in a university memorial tribute, *Justa Edouardo King Naufrago*. Thus by the time he left on his own sea-voyage Milton had, in real terms as adjudged by publication, accomplished very little, not nearly as much as other aspiring young writers such as Randolph or Abraham Cowley, two of the 'more timely happy spirits' to which he had compared himself in Sonnet 7. Cowley had actually published a volume entitled *Poetical Blossoms* in 1633; and by 1631 Randolph had written and/or published several verse plays, including the pastoral drama *Amyntas*, acted before the king and queen in 1631.

Only three years older than Milton, Randolph's prodigious and quite elegant output must have made Milton feel small.

Most of what we know about Milton's Continental tour is thanks to a very retrospective account he himself provided in 1654, in the Latin tract *Defensio Secundo pro Populo Anglicano*, written to explain and defend the English revolution and regicide, and his own role therein. It is devoid of dates but packed with assertions of Milton's respectability and acceptability to European literati, including Giovanni Battista Manso, the famous patron and biographer of Torquato Tasso. In the autobiographical passage in the *Reason of Church Government* Milton described having recited some of his poems to the Italian academicians, their praise reinforcing an 'inward prompting... that by labour and study (which I take to be my portion in this life)' he might indeed become a great poet. He did write a Latin letter of compliment and gratitude to Manso, and a pastoral elegy in Latin for his English friend Charles Diodati, who had been his close companion at Cambridge, but who had died in August 1638, while Milton was abroad. The second was certainly written after Milton's return to London, and the first very probably so. Both, in a sense, were assignments. Both poems, to the delight of Milton scholars, contain statements of an ambition to write a British epic based on Arthurian materials. The statements are all we have. After that there were no signs of poetic activity for several years.

In the *Second Defense* Milton tells us that his plans to visit Sicily and Greece were interrupted by the news from England of 'the civil commotions'—that is, the First Bishops' War against the Scots, declared late in January 1639. Seeing himself in the light of 1654, Milton wrote 'I thought it base to be travelling for amusement abroad, while my fellow-citizens were fighting for liberty at home.' This was an odd description of the war to put down the Scottish rebellion over the imposition of the English prayer-book, and in fact Milton did not immediately return home, but spent several more months in Florence, and visited Venice, where he spent a month sightseeing and buying books. When he eventually returned home, in late July or early August 1639, the war was in abeyance; but the Scots had, significantly, changed the structure of their church government, replacing the hierarchical and ritual structure of episcopacy (bishops at the top) with the somewhat more egalitarian organization of presbytery. Would this model spread to England?

Milton's behavior on his return was consistent with the program of 'labour and intent study' he saw as his future, but had nothing to do with 'the fight for liberty' he later claimed brought him back. He left his family home at Horton for the more professional venue of London, and in the autumn of 1639 or early in 1640 rented lodgings near Fleet Street. He had agreed to take on the education of his two young nephews, John and Edward Phillips, and both the little boys and their uncle began a rigorous program. Milton reopened a notebook he had used at Horton as a record of his reading, and now rapidly filled it with references to, and citations from, new research. This 'Commonplace Book' was already divided into four sections: Ethical, Economic, Political, and a Theological one which has not survived. The new entries show an interest in British history or political thought, especially Holinshed's *Chronicles* (the most frequently quoted work). By 1644 Milton had turned to European history, such as Paolo Sarpi's *Historia del Concilio Tridentino*, to which he makes thirteen references. The Political Index, much the longest, has an overflowing section under the heading 'King' and another under 'Tyrant'. If this were a broad program of humanist reading, as some have posited, it will turn out to have direct political applications. It was not a seedbed for poetry.

It must have been becoming increasingly difficult to ignore what was happening outside the walls of the study and private schoolroom. In 1640 Bishop Joseph Hall responded to the threat of spreading Presbyterianism by publishing *Episcopacie by Divine Right*, a provocative title if ever there were one. In March 1641 five Presbyterian ministers, one of whom, Thomas Young, had been Milton's private tutor, wrote jointly *An Answer* to a second pamphlet by Hall. The *Answer* was followed by an anonymous *Postscript* attacking episcopacy on historical grounds, with references to the English historical sources, Holinshed, Speed, and Stow, that Milton had just been reading. Don Wolfe, the *Postscript's* modern editor, therefore inferred that the anonymous author was John Milton (*CPW* 1: 79–80), not least because in May 1641 there had appeared, also anonymously, another tract in the conflict about the bishops: *Of Reformation Touching Church-Discipline in England*, which was largely an expansion, with some splendid metaphors, of the *Postscript*. This was Milton's entrée into the world of political polemic—for political it was, despite the focus on church affairs. By the early spring of 1642 Milton had written four more tracts against the bishops, to the third of which, the *Reason of Church Government Urg'd against Prelaty*, he put his name. And into it he inserted not only an account of his education and Italian journey, but a long complaint of having been distracted from higher things. He wrote once more about his literary ambitions, how painful he found it to put them aside 'to imbark in a troubl'd sea of noises and hoars disputes' (*CPW* 1: 821), and famously declared that in writing polemic he was only using his left hand.

But embarked he was, and perhaps it was habit-forming. On February 7, 1642, the House of Lords assented to the bill excluding all the bishops from their House, and Milton might reasonably have returned to his 'calme and pleasing solitariness' (1: 821), in the belief that he had marginally contributed to this reform. But what happened next surprised everybody, including, perhaps, Milton himself. In the summer of 1642, just after his fifth anti-prelatical tract appeared, Milton suddenly decided to get married. His choice was at first sight unfortunate (though perhaps it was love at first sight that was to blame). At 33, after a very short courtship, he married Mary Powell, the 18-year-old daughter of Richard Powell, a royalist gentleman in Oxfordshire, who owed Milton a substantial sum of money. For this phase, we have the colorful testimony of Edward Phillips, his nephew and pupil, himself 12 at the time. We can read this testimony in a useful collection of early lives of Milton edited by Helen Darbishire. The young bride, brought back to London, soon became miserable in this rigorously scholarly household, and asked permission to go back to Oxfordshire until the end of September. Meanwhile, the looming civil war between king and parliament had actually broken out. Oxford became a royalist stronghold (with Milton's brother Christopher among the king's supporters). Mary did not return at the appointed time, and her family refused communications with the deserted husband. By January 1643 the House of Commons forbade traffic with Oxford. By August 1, Milton had written the first of four pamphlets advocating a change in England's divorce laws, which were still regulated by canon law. Though he never mentions Mary Milton, we can easily read between the lines of the first divorce pamphlet, the *Doctrine and Discipline of Divorce*, to recover his massive disappointment in his young wife, and his consequent insistence that canon law, by allowing divorce only for adultery or non-consummation, was entirely missing the point. Marriage was always, since Genesis, Milton now argued, intended to be less for sex or procreation than for emotional solace or intellectual support, a meeting of minds.

Between May 1641 and August 1644 Milton had published five pamphlets on church reform, four on reform of the divorce laws; and some of these tracts were long. Suddenly he had become a published author of some standing. That intensive study was still going on was advertised, if not proven, by his publication also of *Of Education* in June 1644, a fearsome account of the pedagogical regime that Milton was presumably attempting on behalf of his nephews. But meanwhile his divorce pamphlets were causing a scandal. The Presbyterians, whose cause Milton thought he had assisted in the church reform pamphlets, were now insisting on the need to control radical or 'wicked' ideas in the marketplace of print. The House of Commons charged a committee to seek out and prosecute the authors, printers, and publishers of 'the Pamphlets against the immortality of the Soul and Concerning Divorce' (*CPW* 2: 142). Everybody knew that the latter referred to Milton, who had signed the preface to the second, expanded edition of the *Doctrine*. William Prynne, whose own cruel treatment by

Charles I for writing against the court had made him a revolutionary hero and martyr, now turned his coat and recommended that the Grand Council should suppress 'Atheistical opinions, as of the soules mortalitie, divorce at pleasure, &c' (2: 142). Any thought that Milton might have had of retiring to 'the quiet and still air of delightfull studies' (1: 822) was put aside by these challenges. The result was, in the eyes of literary scholars, Milton's most brilliant and gorgeous piece of prose, *Areopagitica*, which began merely as an argument against the censorship of books. But self-defense put Milton in a flame which generated larger liberal principles he might not have previously thought through. Despite the occasional cavil (from those who object to Milton's exempting Catholic publications from such freedom), we have made it into one of the founding texts of early modern and modern liberalism. But in late November 1644, it utterly failed to achieve its specific goal, of persuading the Long Parliament to repeal its new licensing Act, which largely reinstated the censorship legislation and mechanisms of Charles I.

Milton now leased a larger house in Cripplegate, apparently with the intention of expanding his school and possibly of marrying again. He was having trouble with his eyesight, and needed domestic help. But in the summer of 1645, reconciliation between Milton and his estranged wife was effected by friends. Mary returned to her husband's house, to help him run what was now a much larger establishment. At this point Milton collected and published almost all his early poems, both in English and in Latin, and worked on several scholarly projects, including a history of Russia (Moscovia), a history of early

Britain, and the textbooks on grammar and logic. Was this a deliberate withdrawal from the political arena, or lack of other opportunities? In 1654 he complained that his polemical skills had received no recognition or reward, whereas 'other men secured offices at no cost to themselves'. 'As for me, no man has ever seen me seeking office,... clinging with suppliant expression to the doors of Parliament' (*CPW* 4: 627). Meanwhile it had become clear that Charles I was losing the civil war, and that the new government would consist of some blend of the Long Parliament with the army leaders, of whom Oliver Cromwell was preeminent. On December 6, 1648 Colonel Pride and his forces arrested or excluded two-thirds of the Presbyterian MPs who had been negotiating with the king. Milton now knew that those in charge were the eighty-odd remaining parliamentarians, who became known as the Rump Parliament. On January 4, 1649, the Rump formally declared the kingdom a republic, and the army leaders determined to try Charles I on a charge of high treason against his subjects. The trial began on January 20, and ten days later the king was executed.

These events shut down Milton's second retreat into pure scholarship. After nearly four years of silence in the public sphere, he suddenly reappeared as the author of a revolutionary pamphlet justifying the king's trial, its title, the *Tenure of Kings and Magistrates*, marking a foray into hard core political theory. Once again, he managed to obscure the motives and the process of this volte-face, by claiming, in 1654, that he wrote as a private citizen, that he had only been drawn to defend the regicides after Charles had already been condemned to death, and that he had had no intention of influencing the trial. The *Tenure* was indeed published after the king's death, on or about February 13, 1649. But it is highly likely that Milton was asked to write something theoretical for the trial, perhaps by John Bradshaw, the presiding judge, whose connections with Milton have been documented by Blair Worden. Milton had to work fast, a talent he had already displayed in his previous bursts of polemic. One reason he was able to do so now was that he could turn back to his 'Commonplace Book', where ready to hand was his Political Index, with its entries on 'The State', 'Laws', 'King', 'Subject', 'The Tyrant', 'Liberty', and 'Various Forms of Government', a virtual textbook of political theory, though as yet undigested. Having been handed a new occasion for the use of his talents (and his notes), Milton rose to it with an energy and eloquence that can still seem shocking, given the nature of the argument.

In March 1649, in obvious exchange for services rendered, Milton was offered one of those 'offices' he later claimed most scrupulously not to have sought: he was made Latin Secretary to the revolutionary Council of State, to write foreign correspondence and the occasional 'official' response to a crisis, such as the royalist threat in Ireland. More importantly, he was commissioned to respond to *Eikon Basilike*, the partly ghost-written defense of the king's conduct and motives during the war, which effectively presented Charles as a martyr. So enormously popular was the 'king's book' that in its first year it sold thirty-five editions in London and twenty-five more in Ireland and Europe. In October or November 1649, Milton was ready with his riposte, *Eikono-klastes*, or the Image-Breaker, a title which attempted to undo the emotional effect of the famous frontispiece to the *Eikon*, picturing the king on his knees, discarding his earthly crown for a heavenly

one. Alas for Milton's reputation, there were only two editions of
Eikonoklastes, a clear sign of where popular sentiment still lay. But
almost immediately he was given a new commission, to reply to
the *Defensio Regio pro Carolo I* by the French scholar Claude de
Saumaise (Salmasius), who took it upon himself to speak for
Europe on the unlawfulness of England's proceedings. Had Salmasius been successful in arousing European intervention, Charles
II might have been returned to the throne by force in 1650, instead
of having to wait another decade. But Milton was able to show the
inadequacy of Salmasius' scholarship and political theory, and
clearly won the argument. That he also mocked the man for
being a hen-pecked husband could perhaps have been anticipated.

In all, Milton wrote three Latin *Defenses* addressed to a
European audience: the first of the English commonwealth
(1651), the second of what had become Cromwell's Protectorate
(1654), and the third, *Pro se Defensio* (1655) of himself and his
polemical conduct, the last of which today seems far from
unblameworthy, not least because he refused to admit that in
the *Second Defense* he had made the massive mistake of attacking the wrong man. The first *Defense* cost him the sight of his
remaining good eye. Milton saw this as a heroic sacrifice for his
principles. The first two *Defenses* established him as the primary
spokesman for the English experiment in government, and
foreigners visited him as a great man. But the *Pro se Defensio*
is a scurrilous personal duel with Alexander More, who had *not*
written *The Cry of the King's Blood*, but who had dared to attack
Milton.

Meanwhile Mary Milton died giving birth to a daughter, and was
shortly followed by their baby son John. A second marriage, to

Katherine Woodcock in 1656, was followed two years later by her death. On the domestic front everything was misery. On the political, there are hints that Milton was disillusioned by the regime he had praised so effusively in the *Second Defense*, and he never attached himself in personal loyalty to Cromwell, the route taken by his friend Andrew Marvell. As the Presbyterians had turned out to be as coercive as the bishops they displaced, so Cromwell, by assuming supreme power in the state, Milton thought, was hardly to be distinguished from the monarch he had executed.

On September 3, 1658, Oliver Cromwell died. From Milton's perspective, for his son Richard to succeed him as Protector was almost as bad as hereditary monarchy. But actual hereditary monarchy was the chief threat. Amid the chaos of political deal-making and breaking, the return of the Rump Parliament, and the appearance of another military leader, General George Monck, Milton braced his 'left hand' once more and wrote two versions of a pamphlet whose very title made a huge challenge: the *Readie & Easie Way to establish a Free Commonwealth; and the Excellence therof Compar'd with the inconveniencies and dangers of readmitting Kingship in this Nation* (1660). No longer under the protection of the Council of State, Milton had to return to the status of independent public intellectual, and face the risks. No printer could be found for the second edition willing to sign his name to it. It appeared just a few days before Charles II himself returned to England.

The year 1660, therefore, was another turning point for Milton, marking his enforced and perhaps truly desired final retreat from controversy. Despite a period of actual danger, when he could have been executed along with other leading regicides, a brief spell in prison, and having to flee his home to escape from the plague and the Great Fire of 1666, he settled into what his early biographers describe as an orderly compositional routine. In 1663 he had solved some of his personal difficulties by a third marriage, to Elizabeth Minshull, a much younger woman who contracted to cook and keep a comfortable house for him. And whether or not he had, as we think, begun *Paradise Lost* in 1658, by 1665 he had an extensive draft of the poem, and by the end of April 1667, a publisher: Samuel Simmons, whose father Matthew had published the *Tenure* and *Eikonoklastes*. When *Paradise Lost* appeared it was immediately recognized as a highly original masterpiece.

But, as usual with Milton, one thing led to another in the same genre. Piqued by a comment by his young Quaker friend and clerical assistant, Thomas Ellwood, that he had for all time defined the loss of Paradise but omitted to describe its restoration, Milton produced to order *Paradise Regained*, which may have originally been written as a play and expanded with epic trappings. Perhaps as an afterthought, the publisher, the redoubtable Whig John Starkey, supplemented this still rather short poem in 1671 with something that was undoubtedly written as a play, though 'never intended for the stage', *Samson Agonistes*.

One major work, so far unmentioned, was also being readied for the press in 1672 or 1673. This was the vast theological treatise, written in Latin, on which Milton had been working sporadically since at least the 1650s, but which had now become, in its early chapters, extremely heterodox. Though based on an orthodox Calvinist tract by John Wolleb (Wollebius), and similarly divided into two books, one on Faith and the other on Works, the first book had grown exponentially, and on the issues of the nature of the Son, the Trinity, and predestination it now bore distinct traces, respectively, of Socinianism, Arianism, and Arminianism. An introductory epistle made it clear that Milton intended publication, but the agent into whose hands it fell, whether by Milton's choice or not, aroused the suspicions of the Dutch printer. The printer alerted the English Secretary of State, and the manuscript ended up in the London Public Record Office, where it was discovered in 1823. Since its nineteenth-century revival, the *De Doctrina Christiana* has continued to obsess Miltonists, some of whom still cannot bear to think that Milton wrote it. But even though it is written in Latin, and about two-thirds of its words are biblical citation, a study of Milton's writing habits, his lexicon, would be incomplete without it.

Finally, as if to summarize his career as disengaged literateur, Milton arranged to have his early poems republished in 1673, adding to them the sonnets he had written since 1645—all but four. Three of these had been written to revolutionary heroes: Sir Thomas Fairfax, Oliver Cromwell, and Sir Henry Vane; the fourth had been addressed to his personal friend Cyriack Skinner, on the subject of Milton's blindness. I lost my eyes, wrote Milton in 1655, 'in liberty's defence, my noble task, | Of which all Europe talks from side to side'. It would take Milton's nephew Edward Phillips, in his 1694 edition of his uncle's state letters, to resurrect these poems as a group. This extraordinary fact of book history (and of self-censorship) often goes unmentioned by Milton's modern scholars, biographers, and editors. Thus the long internal debate between the public figure, who loved the limelight and feared nobody, and the private author/scholar, who felt safer in the ivory tower, had still not yet been resolved.

What does this story tell us, and what will it help to explain? First, it shows us a Milton who, rather than planning his career in the cool environment of the study, mostly wrote in response to immediate stimuli from the outside world. Second, it shows that he usually worked in bursts and clusters, repeating himself until he had exhausted himself: five church reform pamphlets, four divorce pamphlets, three 'defenses', three great poems. For each of these bursts, he developed a new vocabulary, partly original, partly dictated by the conventions of the genre, though no one part of a cluster is quite like the others. Third, it is clear that Milton loved a verbal fight, and that the energies so released allowed him not only to ransack the coffers of his native language but also to fill them with words unfound by others. It follows that he could not have been such a great and original poet had he not been such a great and inventive polemicist. It follows that working with Milton's words is a huge and endless task, for which indefatigability is a help but far from a final solution.

Words of Avoidance: the Divorce Pamphlets

How did Milton arrive at that blissful arrangement of words, 'Love unlibidinous reign'd' to describe the world's first marriage? Not without considerable grief. This chapter leaps over the early poems, and indeed over Milton's first forays into polemic on the side of the Presbyterians, to his four pamphlets advocating a radical change in the divorce laws, of which the first, the *Doctrine and Discipline of Divorce*, is by far the most inventive in its vocabulary, and the most shocking. This was because he was as deeply involved in the issue, personally, as he later became in national politics.

In Milton's Commonplace Book, under the 'Economic Index', his third entry was 'Marriage. See of Divorce'. This very long entry, which seems to have been begun before Milton went on his Continental journey, shows that his first interest in these topics was related to clerical marriage, its contested history both before and after the Reformation, and the problem created when an heir to the throne married someone of another faith. On p. 112 he turned to the topic of divorce, and entered a series of citations from Sarpi, Bodin, and Thuanus (Jacques de Thou). His entries from Sarpi, which may have been made as early as 1641, refer to Sarpi's history of matrimony from Adam onwards, showing its late development into an institution. On p. 114, having run out of space under 'Marriage', and having found more in Thuanus that interested him, he started a new entry. On p. 116, he added a new small entry on 'Divorce' which derives from the physician Sinibaldus, and is surely connected to his new project, conceived in 1642, to rewrite the rules of marriage and divorce for his own country. The entry is worth citing:

> The reason why [divorce] ought to be permitted is that, as physicians and almost all others acknowledge, [copulation] without love is cold, unpleasant, unfruitful, harmful, bestial, abominable. Sinibald: *Geneanthropeais* Book 1, tractate 2. The preface. *Therefore it is intolerable that either one or at least the innocent one should be bound unwillingly by so monstruous a fetter.*
>
> (*CPW* 1: 414; italics added)

Ruth Mohl, the editor of the Commonplace Book for the Yale edition of Milton's prose, commented that the conclusion (italicized here) was Milton's own thinking, but she did not remark on *monstruous*, which strikes us even today as excessive.

It is unusual for a commonplace book to contain an entry on divorce, though this was a topic discussed by Bodin, whom Milton consulted. What these entries show is that Milton's thoughts on marriage and divorce were originally political in nature, and only became personal at about the time when, as Edward Phillips later told the story, Milton's own marriage to Mary Powell seemed to have ended in humiliating circumstances. When he first committed himself to writing about this topic, Milton was anxious not to seem personally involved in the matter. In the supplementary address to the Long Parliament that he added for the second edition of the *Doctrine and Discipline of Divorce* he warned of the possibility of being 'traduc't to be the agent of his owne by-ends, under pretext of Reformation' (*CPW* 2: 225); and in the *Second Defense* he notoriously argued, retroactively, that his divorce pamphlets were merely part of a disinterested analysis of the 'three varieties of liberty without which civilized life is scarcely possible', that is, religious, domestic, and civil liberties. Even in that supplementary address, however, Milton soon conceded that there may be something in the underlying structure of self-interest that can be turned to everyone's advantage: 'Yet when points of difficulty are to be discuss, appertaining to the removal of unreasonable wrong and burden from the perplex life of our brother, it is incredible how cold, how dull, and farre from all fellow-feeling we are, without the spurre of self-concernment' (2: 226). And if one stays with the passage in the *Second Defense* past the three high-minded categories of liberty to be defended, one finds Milton remarking that 'it is to little purpose to make a noise about liberty in the legislative assemblies... who is in bondage to an inferior at home—a species of bondage of all others the most degrading to a man'. 'Him', 'who', 'a man', 'our brother'. All these syntactical diversions were swung into place to protect Milton from the charge of arguing for his own divorce, or from engaging in covert autobiography.

B Y - E N D S . This odd and rare word, which means 'secret selfish purposes', would reappear in 1678 as the name of a disreputable character in Bunyan's *Pilgrim's Progress*, one of the many false professors of religion who cannot be saved. Yet it is precisely the fact of having by-ends of his own that Milton admits by making this disclaimer. To support this claim, I will dwell both on the various grammatical, especially pronominal, strategies that Milton developed to keep himself out of the picture, and on the strange set of euphemisms or periphrases he invented to keep sex itself at some sort of verbal distance.

But first we need to revisit the biographical 'facts' of his first marriage as recounted much later, in 1694, by his nephew Edward Phillips, who had been one of the members of Milton's household in London. 'About Whitsuntide [in 1642]', Phillips tells us, 'Milton took a Journey into the Country: no body about him certainly knowing the Reason, or that it was any more than a Journey of Recreation.' What follows has many of the contours of romantic fiction-surprise, social detail, a severe breach in the marriage, and a carefully crafted reconciliation. 'After a Month's stay,' Phillips continued:

> Home he returns a Married-man, that went out a Batchelor. His wife being Mary, the eldest daughter of Mr. Richard Powell, then a justice of the peace of Forresthill, near Shotover in Oxfordshire; some few of her nearest relations accompanying the bride to her new habitation; which by reason [Milton's] father nor any body else were yet come, was able to receive them; where the feasting held for some days in celebration of the nuptials and for entertainment of the bride's friends. At length they took their leave and returning to Forresthill left the sister

behind, probably not much to her satisfaction as appeared by the sequel. By that time she had for a Month or thereabout led a Philosophical Life (after having been used to a great House, and much Company and Joviality), her friends, possibly incited by her own desire, made earnest suit by Letter, to have her company the remaining part of the Summer, which was granted on condition of her return at the time appointed, Michaelmas, or thereabout.   (Darbishire, p. 64)

Reading between the lines of his account, we can see that Phillips has intimated the stress, in terms both of money and space, that Milton must have experienced in putting up the wedding party 'for some days', until 'at length' they went home. He was, after all, living in lodgings rented from a tailor, in St. Bride's Churchyard, which were unlikely to be spacious. What Phillips does not tell us is the youth of the bride (Mary Powell was 18 when she married, whereas Milton was 33), but everything else necessary for our understanding of the plot Phillips gives us: the clash between the cheerful life in a big country house that the bride had hitherto experienced ('much Company and Joviality') and the 'Philosophical Life' (the capitalization is revealing) she was now expected to live with her schoolmaster husband; the egregious mistake that was made on both sides when the bride was allowed to run home for the rest of the summer, rather than husband and wife coming to terms with their differences.

Michaelmas comes on September 29. Between the middle of June, let's say, and the end of September, Milton, Phillips tells us, was 'now as it were a single man again', an extraordinary locution. One of the ways he spent his time was in visiting Lady Margaret Lee, a married woman of 'great wit and ingenuity', who enjoyed Milton's company, as did her husband, Colonel Hobson. Milton wrote Lady Margaret a sonnet, and paid her the great compliment of including her name in it. But 'Michaelmas being come and no news of his Wife's return', Phillips continued:

> [Milton] sent for her by Letter; and receiving no answer, sent several other Letters, which were also unanswered; so that at last he dispatch'd down a Foot-Messenger with a Letter, desiring her return; but the Messenger came back not only without an answer, at least a satisfactory one, but to the best of my remembrance, reported that he was dismissed with some sort of Contempt.

Phillips speculated that the cause of Mary's failure to return was in part political; the royalist Powells, with the King's party established at Oxford, imagined that the civil war would soon be ended in their favor, and that the marriage would become 'a blot in their Escutcheon'. But he also recorded Milton's state of mind at this treatment:

> It so incensed our Author, that he thought it would be dishonourable ever to receive her again, after such a repulse; so that he forth prepared to Fortify himself with Arguments for such a Resolution, and accordingly wrote...Treatises, by which he undertook to maintain, That it was against Reason, and...not proveable by

scripture, for any Married Couple disagreeable in Hu-
mour and Temper, or having an aversion to each other,
to live yok'd together all their Days.

Here, then, and not in any disinterested overview of the vital
human liberties, lay the motive for both editions of the *Doctrine
and Discipline of Divorce* (August 1, 1643 and February 2, 1644),
followed by the three more tracts that Milton felt he needed to
defend himself against the hostile reaction to the first: The
Judgement of Martin Bucer (July 15, 1644), sparked by Milton's
late discovery that the German reformer had preceded him in
making such arguments; *Tetrachordon* (March 4, 1645), Milton's most comprehensive attempt to deal with what Scripture
had to say on the subject of divorce; and *Colasterion* (March 4,
1645), a diatribe against the anonymous author of *An Answer to
a Book, Intituled, The Doctrine and Discipline of Divorce, or, A
Plea for Ladies and Gentlewomen, and all other Maried Women
against Divorce*. This attack on Milton had appeared from the
press in November 1644, with an egregious note added by the
licenser, Joseph Caryl, to the effect that he licensed the work 'To
preserve the strength of the Marriage-bond and the Honour of
that estate against those sad breaches and dangerous abuses of it
which common discontents (on this side Adultery) are likely to
make in unstaid minds and men given to change'.

This is a great deal of compositional activity and research to
have been generated by one traumatic marriage, and somewhat
disproportionate to the role of public intellectual that Milton
now claimed. But Milton, Phillips told us, was 'incensed'. And
the more incensed he was, the more high-minded he wished to

sound (although *Colasterion*, which is almost pure vituperation, is the exception). To understand his frustration, we need to understand what the legal situation was at the time.

In mid-seventeenth-century England the legislation governing marriage was out of date, considering that England was supposed to have joined the Reformation. English marriages were still governed by canon law, which decreed, since marriage was a sacrament, that there could be no divorce with right of remarriage, no complete freedom *a vinculo matrimoniae*, from the chains of matrimony. What was possible was legal separation (*a mensa et thoro*), freedom to eat and sleep alone. The grounds, however, were narrow, being limited in England to adultery and cruelty. Canon law permitted nullification on the grounds of a prior cause unknown to one of the partners, such as consanguinity, a prior contract, impotence, or female impenetrability. In Europe most Protestant states, denying that marriage was a sacrament, recognized remarriage for the innocent party after divorce for adultery. In 1552 Edward VI had appointed a commission to bring England into line with Continental practice; the commission had included Archbishop Thomas Cranmer and Sir John Cheke, and the product was the Reformatio Legum Ecclesiasticarum, a set of proposals for reform which included divorce for desertion and for 'capital hatreds' (*CPW* 2: 717). The proposals had been defeated, however, in the House of Commons, and under Elizabeth and James the Anglican hierarchy reinforced the position of canon law. Yet, privately, reform ministers ignored the canons and recognized marriages of the innocent party in cases of adultery or desertion, the latter being Milton's case. Milton might have begun collecting arguments about divorce 'to Fortify' himself for making such a request. He started, Phillips tells us, to hope to marry again, 'one of Dr. Davis's daughters, a very handsome and witty gentlewoman'. But by the time he had worked through the arguments, he apparently believed he could single-handedly persuade the Long Parliament and the Westminster Assembly to change the law in Reformation England—to legislate the right to divorce *a vinculo* for both parties, not only on the old grounds, but also for incompatibility. Hence his concern to be seen taking the high ground, and not suspected of being the agent 'of his own by-ends'. In his plan for reform he was hopelessly unrealistic. Although by the time of his *second* marriage regulation of the institution had been removed from canon law and made a civil matter, such expanded grounds for divorce would not be legislated in England until more than half way through the twentieth century. And in his hopes of appearing disinterested, he actually sent up linguistic smoke signals of distress.

Milton approached his topic both high-mindedly and high-handedly, by redefining a true marriage as the marriage of minds, not bodies. Canon law focused only on adultery or non-consummation. For Milton, this was to utterly misunderstand the institution of marriage as created by God and described in Genesis. Now that he had started on this argument, Milton had come to believe that marriage was the source of human happiness. When St. Paul made that ungenerous concession, 'It is better to marry then to burne,' he had failed to understand the words of Genesis. 'What might this burning mean?' asks Milton. 'Certainly not the meer motion of carnall lust, nor the meer goad of a sensitive desire':

What is it then but that desire which God put into Adam in Paradise...that desire which God saw it was not good that man should be left alone to burn in; the desire and longing to put off an unkindly solitarines by uniting another body, but not without a fit soule to his in the cheerful society of wedlock. Which if it were so needful before the fall, when man was much more perfect in himself, how much more is it needful now against all the sorrows and casualties of this life to have an intimate and speaking help, a ready and reviving associate in marriage...*Who* hath the power to struggle with an intelligible flame, not in Paradise to be resisted, become now more ardent, by being fail'd of what in reason it lookt for.   (*CPW* 2: 251–52)

Thus, under the sign of the universal 'Who' who must remain nameless, Milton discovered for himself the concept of companionate marriage as Protestantism was still inventing it, and the engine of his discovery was humiliation and disappointment. That is to say, by finding Mary Milton wanting (and missing), he imagined from the hole she had made in his feelings what a good marriage might be. Consequently he could see for himself what was wrong with a legal system that encouraged hypocrisy, stressed the dynastic and physical aspects of marriage over the psychological and sociable, and did not allow for second chances.

HE WHO. Long after Milton's marriage went wrong, Edward Phillips, as we have seen, told this as a story with psychological depth and interest, making it clear that Milton's primary motive in writing the divorce pamphlets was his personal discomfiture. But from the start a careful (or suspicious) reader of this tract would have seen that it tells unintentionally a personal story. In Book 1, Chapter 3, Milton seeks to refute the argument that divorce would be unnecessary if people carefully considered the 'disposition' of their intended mates beforehand. 'But let them know again', Milton responded to this unheard objection:

> that for all the warinesse can be us'd, it may yet befall a discreet man to be mistak'n in his choice: [and we have plenty of examples]. The soberest and best govern'd men are lest practiz'd in these affairs: and *who knows not* that the bashfull muteness of a virgin may oft-times hide all the unlivelines & naturall sloth which is really unfit for conversation; nor is there that freedom of accesse granted or presum'd, as may suffice to a perfect discerning until too late; and where any indisposition is suspected, what more usuall then the perswasion of friends, that acquaintance, as it increases, will amend all: And lastly, it is not strange though many who have spent their youth chastely, are in some things not so quick-sighted, while they hast too eagerly to light the nuptiall torch.
>
> (*CPW* 2: 249; italics added)

This is a brilliant rendering of one possible outcome of the sociology of early modern courtship, told with rather more circumstantial detail than readers might expect, turned into a paradigm by that clever 'who knows not'. And instead of considering other possible narratives—as say, the dowry is not

forthcoming, the bride loves another—Milton continues to fill
in the character of the anonymous misguided bridegroom:

> Since they who have liv'd most loosely by reason of their
> bold accustoming, prove most successfull in their
> matches, because their wild affections unsettling at will,
> have been as so many divorces to teach them experience.
> When as the sober man honouring the appearance of
> modestie, and hoping well of every sociall virtue under
> that veile, may easily chance to meet, if not with a body
> impenetrable, yet often with a minde to all other due
> conversation inaccessible, and to all the more estimable
> and superior purposes of matrimony useless and almost
> liveles.   (*CPW* 2: 249–50)

The phrase added in the second edition ('and we have plenty of
examples') was obviously intended by Milton to deflect attention
from himself as the most obvious sober man in sight, the one
who had written *Il Penseroso* and the *Masque at Ludlow*, and
acknowledged being mocked at Cambridge as too pure for pranks.
A supporting strategy of self-concealment is the use of adverbs
implying a broader spectrum: 'oft-times', 'usuall', 'many', 'often'.

The would-be divorcer, invariably referred to as male, is not
only sober but melancholy to a fault. Having mischosen his mate,
he is far worse off than the single man, for 'here the continuall
sight of his deluded thoughts without cure, must needs be to him,
if especially his complexion incline him to melancholy, a daily
trouble and paine of losse in some degree like that which Repro-
bates feel' (*CPW* 2: 247). Even though qualified by 'in some
degree', this remark is truly horrifying, allying the incautious

husband with those ordained by God to damnation. And in the same passage Milton unintentionally emphasized his own sexual reticence, by arguing that the same 'sober man' shall 'do more manly, to be extraordinary and singular in claiming the due right whereof he is frustrate, then to piece up his lost contentment by visiting the Stews, or stepping to his neighbours bed, which is the common shift in this misfortune' (2: 247).

This story is further complicated by two rival narratives of female unacceptability. One appears in the narrative of unwise courtship, when the 'bashfull muteness of a virgin' conceals the 'unlivelines & naturall sloth which is really unfit for conversation' (2: 249), from which we might infer that Mary was reticent, untalkative, ill-educated. The other appears much later in the pamphlet when Milton confronts the argument made by Beza and Paraeus, that the Mosaic dispensation for divorce was awarded for the protection of wives against the cruelty of husbands. 'Palpably uxurious!' exclaimed Milton at this point (Book 2, Chapter 15), in one of the most dramatic utterances of the entire work:

> *Who can be ignorant* that woman was created for man, and not man for woman; and that a husband may be injur'd as insufferably in marriage as a wife. What an injury is it after wedlock not to be belov'd, what to be slighted, what to be contended with in point of house-rule who shall be head, nor for any parity of wisdom, for that were something reasonable, but out of female pride.   (*CPW* 2: 234)

This list of injuries conjures up a number of domestic scenes, of which 'not to be belov'd' is the most poignant, but 'to be contended with in point of house-rule' the most readily imaginable. Milton then inserted into the second edition of the tract an obscure scriptural anecdote from the book of Esther (1: 10–22), of 'the cours which the Medes and Persians took by occasion of Vashti, whose meer denial to come at her husbands sending lost her the being Queen any longer'. It cannot be a coincidence that this tale matches the one told by Edward Phillips, as to how Mary Powell, or her family, ignored Milton's letters requiring his wife's return. Here the wife is defined as not passively uncommunicative but actively rebellious against her lord and husband.

'What an injury is it after wedlock not to be belov'd' is actually a strange outburst in this context, in which 'not to be *obeyed*' would have made more sense. I hear in it an uncontrollable echo of an earlier passage in which Milton introduced the paradox that the would-be divorcer is actually the best upholder of marriage. 'For to retain still', he wrote,

> and not to be able to love, is to heap up more injury . . . **He who** therefore who lacking of his due in the most native and humane end of marriage, thinks it better to part then to live sadly and injuriously to that cherfull covnant (for not to be belov'd & yet retain'd, is the greatest injury to a gentle spirit) **he I say who** therefore seeks to part, is one who highly honours the married life, and would not stain it.   (*CPW* 2: 253)

Even if we have long abandoned Freud as the key to all mythologies, it is difficult to find a better word than Freudian for the slippage (apparently invisible to Milton) from the high-minded 'to retain still and not to be able to love', to the elegiac (and soon to be echoed) 'not to *be* belov'd and yet retain'd'. Who, this syntax forces us to ask, is doing the divorcing and at what moment does it occur? At the failure of love, or at the formal separation? Who injures whom? Does the chiasmus indicate a moment of gender parity in Milton's thinking, or rather the hideous recognition that when he thought he was in control (retaining, but unable to love) he was in fact himself obliged by the law to remain a prisoner, retained and unloved?

The 'he who' as a substitute for the first person singular is a device that Milton used throughout his career. In the church reform pamphlets it registers a heroic, crusading persona. To some extent this persona survives into the *Doctrine*, as in 'hee who shall endeavour the amendment of any old neglected grievance in Church or State' (*CPW* 2: 224) or 'he who wisely would restrain the reasonable Soul of man within due bounds' (2: 227). Both of these were built into the new address to Parliament added in 1644. More clearly heroic is this sentence: 'He who by adventuring shall be so happy as with successe ... to light the way of such an expedient liberty and truth as this ... [and] shall deserve to be reck'nd among the publick benefactors of civill and humane life' (2: 239–40). Here, in fact, Milton changed the 'He that' of 1643 to 'He who' in 1644, one of those miniscule alterations that would seem to carry no significance unless perceived as structural. But alongside these heroic standard-bearers we can now place the figure of 'he who marries' and 'intends as little to conspire his own ruine, as he that swears Allegiance' (2: 229), and, most strikingly, in the tangled sentence above, 'He therefore who lacking of his due ... he I say who therefore seeks to part'. This is the grammar of self-division.

PERIPHRASIS. Hanging over the divorce pamphlets, and thanks to Milton's own silence on the subject, there has been a suggestion that the 'real' reason for the desertion and attempted divorce was sexual, that Mary Powell refused to let Milton consummate the marriage. But in 1978 Edward Le Comte, in *Milton and Sex*, a short book with a deliberately shocking title, collected some of the metaphors Milton employs to denote human heterosexual activity in the *Doctrine and Discipline of Divorce*. Le Comte concluded that these metaphors, or periphrases, registered Milton's 'disgust or scorn', and suggested that if the divorce pamphlets 'reflect a sexual refusal, they reflect one, or an inclination to one, far more likely to have come from the husband'. Le Comte noted that Milton equates heterosexual sex not only with animalism—'a bestial necessity', 'bestial burning', 'animal or beastish meeting', 'a brutish congress'—but also with physical labor and slavery. Central to this perception is a sentence Milton added to the 1644 edition: 'that to grind in the mill of an undelighted and servil copulation, must be the only forc't work of a Christian marriage, oft times with such a yokefellow, from whom both love and peace, both nature and Religion mourns to be separated' (*CPW* 1: 258). To put it plainly, this metaphor, 'to grind in the mill', as a way of thinking about a man's making love to a woman, suggests that Milton, a virgin before his marriage, found real-life sexual activity less of a treat than a chore.

Milton's words tell us that he had at this stage of his life considerable trouble with the facts of sexual activity. Sometimes there is a vaguely agricultural veil drawn over them when he speaks of sowing 'the furrow of man's nativity' (*CPW* 2: 270). Sometimes there is merely euphemism, as in 'the vessel of voluptuous enjoyment' or the 'channell of concupiscence' (2: 248–49). But the libidinal narrative—the one that underlies the story of failed romance—cannot decide whether failure or success is more depressing. 'The impediment of carnall performance', the 'stops or extinguish'd … veins of sensuality', and the 'disappointing of an impetuous nerve' alternate with the 'impatience of a sensuall desire … reliev'd', and the 'prescribed satisfaction of an irrational heat'. The canon law prescribes that 'the contract shall stand as firme as ever', no matter how 'flat and melancholious' the emotional relationship. It is the most 'injurious and unnaturall tribute that can be extorted from a person endewed with reason, to be made pay out the best substance of his body, and of his soul too, as some think' (2: 271). So Milton entertained the fear that male ejaculation was bad for you, both physically and intellectually. Above all, in the notorious 'quintessence of an excrement' (2: 248), his periphrasis for semen, Milton rather highlighted than solved the problem of which euphemism is the sign or symptom. Abstract thought and philosophical idealism (expressed in a classicizing and pseudoscientific vocabulary) reveal their connections to a venerable tradition of misogynistic distaste.

In sum, then, the *Doctrine and Discipline of Divorce* presents a logical case for reform of the divorce law, superimposed on a subtext of emotional chaos. Milton could not apparently decide whether his wife deserved to be divorced primarily because of her desertion and disobedience, or because she had disappointed him by her lack of intellectual substance; 'if not with a body impenetrable, yet … with a minde to all other due conversation inaccessible' (2: 250). His writing tells us both that the physical relationship had been established, and that it made him mighty uncomfortable. These sexual tics and grimaces were to disappear, *almost* completely, from his later divorce pamphlets; and part of the reason for the change is that Milton was diverted from resentment against his wife to indignation about the hostile responses to the *Doctrine and Discipline*, in whose reception he now perceived his honor to inhere. The later pamphlets keep unintentional autobiography at bay, in part by relying on the words of Martin Bucer, in part by setting the great scriptural texts on the topic against each other in *Tetrachordon*, in part by displacing disgust onto his adversary in *Colasterion*, 'this fleamy clodd of an Antagonist', who stands in for the female 'image of earth and fleam' (2: 254) that he had, in his initial rage, verbally if not legally discarded.

But of course we are not finished with the story of the Miltons. Edward Phillips himself had continued it, by relating how, given 'the declining state of the King's Cause', efforts were made by the Powells and their friends to effect a reconciliation between the estranged husband and wife. This too has the shape of domestic fiction:

> At last this device was pitch'd upon. There dwelt in the Lane of St. Martins le Grand, which was hard by, a Relation of our Author's, one Blackborough, whom it was known he often visited, and upon this occasion the visits were more narrowly observ'd, and possibly there might be a Combination between both Parties; the Friends on both sides concentring in the same action, though on different behalfs. One time above the rest, he was making his usual

> visit, the Wife was ready in another Room, and on a sudden
> he was surprised to see one whom he thought to have never
> seen more, making Submission and begging Pardon on her
> Knees before him; he might probably at first make some
> shew of aversion and rejection; but partly his own generous
> nature, more inclinable to Reconciliation than to persever-
> ance in Anger and Revenge; and partly the strong inter-
> cession of Friends on both sides, soon brought him to an
> Act of oblivion and a firm League of Peace for the future.
>
> (Darbishire, pp. 66–67)

Phillips's language for the reconciliation is political. Milton's
own description of the scene came many years later, in *Paradise
Lost*, where after the Fall, the first libidinous sex, and the first
human quarrel, Eve returns to Adam and begs his pardon for
her role in their disaster. 'He might probably at first make some
show of aversion and rejection,' Phillips had imagined; and
Milton made Adam's first response be rejection: 'Out of my
sight, thou Serpent.' This speech ends in classical misogyny, in
which Adam wishes for a world without women, a world filled
'With Men as Angels without Feminine', in which God would
have had to find 'some other way to generate Mankind' (*PL* 10:
891–95). But Eve, 'not so repulst, with Tears that ceas'd not
flowing, | And tresses all disorder'd, at his feet | Fell humble,
and imbracing them, besought his peace' (10: 910–12).

Who could resist? Naturally, Adam 'relented | Towards her,
his life so late and sole delight, | Now at his feet submissive in
distress' (10: 939–41). *Colasterion* was published in March 1645.
By October, Mary was living with her husband in his large new

house in the Barbican, and immediately became pregnant with their first daughter.

PISTRINUM. But Milton's thoughts on divorce were not yet a thing of the past. After Mary Milton died, in 1652, he remained a widower until November 1656, when he and Katherine Woodcock were married by a justice of the peace. It is part of the Milton myth that this was the one of his three marriages that was genuinely happy, capable of being described in the ideal terms of the *Doctrine and Discipline*. Tending to that myth are those who read Milton's sonnet, 'Methought I saw my late espoused Saint' as honoring Katherine, who died in February 1658. It is not impossible, however, that the poem was written for Mary. Because Milton refused to name the wife in question, we will never know. What we do know is that, when Milton again took up serious work on the *De Doctrina Christiana*, he devoted a whole chapter of the treatise to the subject of marriage, polygamy, and divorce, no less than twenty pages of the manuscript. (By comparison, the huge topic of Predestination is only given twenty-three pages). More strikingly, however, given that Milton was working on the foundation of John Wolleb's *Abridgment of Christian Divinitie*, is that this topic had no basis in his model. Milton inserted his late thoughts of marriage and divorce into his borrowed structure by tucking it into one of Wolleb's subsections, 'Of the government of man', which logically follows 'Of the government of angels'. In Milton's hugely expanded version, Chapter X carried the heading 'De Gubernatione speciali hominis ante lapsum: ubi etiam de sabbatho et coniugio' (Of the special government of Man before the Fall, including [the Institutions] of the Sabbath and of Marriage). You can see how Sumner's translation in the Columbia edition attempts to validate this extraordinary insertion.

An anonymous early biographer states that Milton began to work on the final stage of *De Doctrina Christiana* after he had written the *Pro se Defensio*, that is, in 1655. The section on marriage and divorce belongs to that part of the manuscript (the first fourteen chapters) which were retranscribed by Daniel Skinner, presumably because the Picard script had been rendered illegible (to a potential publisher) by many revisions. Milton now returns to John Selden's *Uxor Hebraica*, which he had consulted for the Commonplace Book (*CPW* 1: 403), and in the same breath refers back to his own divorce tracts, a neat piece of self-justification: 'ut nos alias ex aliquot scripturae locis et Seldenus idem docuit' (*CE* 15: 172; 'as Selden proves, and as I have myself shown in another treatise from several texts of Scripture'). Selden is needed to provide the broadest possible definition of the word 'fornication', and to distinguish it clearly from 'adultery'.

Nothing much seems to have changed in Milton's argument, except that its vocabulary, as one might expect, has been almost completely pruned of emotion. There is one moment, however, in which old habits break through. We are called by God, Milton writes, to peace; 'non ergo ut perpetuis discordiis et vexationibus conflictemur. Ad pacem enim et libertatem, non ad matrimonium vocamur; multo minus ad infelicis matrimonii perpetuam discordiam et servitutis pistrinum' (*CE* 15: 174; 'We are called to peace and liberty, not to marriage; still less to the perpetual discord of marriage and the grinding-mill of servitude'.) Sumner translated this last phrase, *servitutis pistrinum*, as 'slavish bondage', but John Carey, translating for the Yale edition of the prose, is surely right in choosing 'pounding mill'. *Pistrinum* stands out in sharp contrast to its surroundings. It is a metaphor we have seen before, in the 'grinding in the mill' of the *Doctrine and Discipline*. Lewis and Short define *pistrinum* as 'a place where corn is pounded, a pounding mill, usually worked by horses or asses; but sometimes a lazy or otherwise bad slave was forced to perform this labor'. And that is how Milton used it in the *First Defense*, where he warns Salmasius that he is a perfect candidate for slavery in a state where the citizens are themselves free: ('servitutis candidatum dedere in pistrinum debebit', *CE* 8: 85). The verbal echo of both earlier tracts is yet one more piece of evidence that Milton was indeed the author of *De Doctrina Christiana*.

Did Milton write this passage in the *De Doctrina Christiana* during his few years as a widower, or after his remarriage? We will never know. But for those readers (like myself) who incline to a sentimental connection between the story of the world's first marriage, as retold in *Paradise Lost*, and the story of Milton's first marriage, the existence of this material in the *De Doctrina* is itself a cautionary tale.

Keywords

This chapter deals with some of Milton's keywords. I use the term 'keyword' partly in the sense that Raymond Williams used it, sociologically, to denote the power words in play in any culture at specific times. Williams's own definition of a keyword was that it must be strong, difficult, and persuasive, and in everyday usage; or, alternatively, keywords were 'significant, indicative words in certain forms of thought'. As it turned out, many of Williams's chosen words were more academic than truly demotic, in play on the street, but one of the 'forms of thought' to which keywords pointed in this pioneering work was politics. In the 1970s such words preeminently included: Capitalism, Class, Communism, Democracy, Labour, Liberal, Masses, Radical, Reform, Socialist, Unemployment, Violence, Wealth, and Work.

Keywords are usually abstract nouns, or nouns with a strong tendency towards abstraction, and they tend to provoke a reaction, positive or negative, in the audience. This was just as true in mid-seventeenth-century England. A comparable list for Milton's culture would include: Commonwealth, Democracy, Heresy, King, Justice, Liberty, Monarchy, the People, Prerogative,

Right, Slavery, Schism, Toleration, Tyranny. Milton not only deployed the keywords of seventeenth-century culture, especially political culture, but created some of his own. Looking for keywords in Milton, as distinct from in the language generally, involves counting; but you must only count the words that count; that is to say, words that were inherently, historically, weighty, and on which Milton puts his own intellectual pressure. In Milton, keywords turn out quite literally to be keys to his concerns, and they change as those concerns alter. Here we will investigate three words not in the above list that Milton decided to elevate into keywords, 'Book', 'Truth', and 'Schism' in *Areopagitica*, and four that he pulled out of his environment and turned into pillars of his program: 'Liberty', 'Commonwealth', and 'the People' in the *Readie & Easie Way*, 'Heresy' in *Of True Religion*.

Areopagitica

THE BOOK AND THE TRUTH. The modern reader, unfamiliar with Milton, might well say, like those early readers who objected to the title of *Tetrachordon*: 'Bless us! What a word | on a title page is this!' Harder to pronounce, and even more ostentatiously learned, the title of Milton's address to the Long Parliament in 1644 seems now, and must have seemed then, a barrier between the ordinary reader and comprehension. It takes long learned footnotes to explain, and even when we swallow the allusion to the seventh oration of Isocrates to the Areopagus, a speech which carried a message almost the reverse of Milton's, we are no further ahead. If it were not for the subtitle, 'A Speech For the Liberty of Unlicenc'd Printing', we might very well give up and leave it on the bookstall.

Areopagitica is the one prose tract that has most elevated Milton's reputation since his own time, though its effect in his day was negligible. The divorce tracts made a splash, indeed a scandal, and he felt the need to explain them away, in the *Second Defense*, as part of a more noble project. Now they seem interestingly obsessive and argumentatively specious. The regicide tracts made him an invaluable spokesman for the Commonwealth, and internationally famous, but if we are truthful there is much in them to detest, as well as much to admire. The *Second Defense*, as we shall see in a later chapter, is valuable now primarily for its autobiographical passages, and the lexical ways in which they reveal more than Milton intended. But *Areopagitica* stands as a monument to the slow growth of liberal thought. This has been achieved, to some extent, by scholarly sleight of hand. It is often described as one of the great defenses of the freedom of the press, despite the fact that all Milton argued against was pre-licensing, professing himself quite willing to have books suppressed and burned *after* they had been subject to public scrutiny. At least so he said. How he felt about the burning of his regicide tracts in August 1660 we will never know, but he and his friends would presumably have been willing to see the books executed in symbolic substitution for himself.

Areopagitica has also been subsumed under the Whiggish narrative whereby it is seen primarily as an argument for religious toleration, the conceptual bridge between the Dissenters of the 1640s like Roger Williams, Henry Robinson, John Lilburne, and William Walwyn, who feared that the Presbyterians were setting up a new repressive church government, and the *Letters concerning Toleration* of John Locke. During the Restoration the word 'toleration' was widely used to refer to state policy, but in the 1640s the phrase was usually 'freedom of conscience' or 'liberty of conscience'. By the time he wrote the *Readie & Easie Way to establish a Free Commonwealth* in early 1660 Milton was prepared to erect 'liberty of conscience' into one of the two principles that made up the Good Old Cause, the other of course being republican government. But in *Areopagitica* Milton is mainly concerned with what he calls (and his European friends envy) '*Philosophic* freedom' (*CPW* 2: 537), intellectual freedom, the right to read, study, learn, and argue new ideas in public. Never in the tract does he use the phrase 'liberty of conscience'; instead he demands 'the liberty to know, to utter, and to argue freely according to conscience, above all liberties' (560). 'According to conscience', yes; but this freedom would cover infinitely more than freedom of religious conscience, usually defined as a private matter, the absence of coerced uniformity of worship.

It is true that as Milton begins his peroration he steers it a little more in the direction of religion, under the influence of Lord Brooke, whose *Discourse of Episcopacie* Milton cites directly: 'He there exhorts us to hear with patience and humility those . . . that desire to live purely, in such a use of Gods Ordinances, as the best guidance of their conscience gives them, and to tolerat them, though in some discontinuity to our selves' (561). This is the first time that Milton has ever used the word 'tolerate' in this sense, and the momentum from Brooke's treatise, which Milton obviously has before him as he writes, leads to a stronger and now more famous sentence: 'this doubtless is more wholesome, more prudent, and more Christian that many be tolerated, rather than all compell'd' (565).

But Milton did not set out to write a speech concerning religious toleration. He set out to protest the Long Parliament's Order of June 14, 1643, restoring the system of pre-licensing that had been in force under Charles I, the only difference being that its officers were not to be appointed by the Archbishop of Canterbury and/or the Bishop of London, and that it was no longer a decree of the hated Star Chamber. His motives were primarily personal; the system of licensing offended him as an insult to his intelligence, and perhaps he felt that he had partially provoked the Order by publishing the *Doctrine and Discipline of Divorce* without a license. Herbert Palmer's sermon to the Long Parliament (which *was* explicitly anti-tolerationist) had in turn provoked Milton by calling the *Doctrine* a 'wicked booke', and recommending that it should be burned (*CPW* 2: 103 n.) and much of *Areopagitica* is concerned with how and why a book might be considered 'wicked'. What Milton set out to do was to talk about books, about the book trade, and about the history and mechanics of licensing. At this level his tract belonged less to the history of religion than to what we now call the material history of the book.

This I shall now demonstrate by counting. *Areopagitica* contains 103 appearances of the word 'book' or 'books'. This sets it quite apart from the tracts of Williams, Robinson, Walwyn, or Brooke, the last two of which Milton actually read, and with which it was grouped by Ernest Sirluck in his otherwise invaluable introduction. It also sets it apart from anything else that Milton wrote. The nearest any other tract comes to harping on the word 'book' is *Eikonoklastes*, where, unsurprisingly, given that Milton is refuting the king's own book, it appears 54 times. But, you will counter, what about the word 'Truth', which is wielded with such magnificent force, and is what most readers of *Areopagitica* will remember? It is true that 'Truth' is one of the keywords of *Areopagitica*, and often at the center of some brilliant metaphor. But it is more true that 'Truth' is an afterthought, especially in its grand form as an abstraction. 'Truth' appears 46 times, less than half as many as 'book', and only begins to dominate the discussion two-thirds of the way through the pamphlet, on p. 26 of a forty-page quarto. Let us follow this pattern more closely.

Milton starts by assuming that the intent of the parliamentary Order is to suppress only 'scandalous, seditious, and libelous Books', as stated in its text, though he leaves out their other category, unlicensed publications generally. This leads him to focus on 'how Bookes demeane themselves, as well as men', a quaintly anthropomorphical notion, which alone would justify treating them as malefactors. In the next paragraph, however, he introduces, three times, the concept of the 'good Booke' as more valuable to society than a man's life. On p. 4 he has used this keyword 7 times. Then, when he launches into the history of censorship from antiquity onwards, 'book' and 'books' appear more often than is strictly necessary for the argument. On p. 6 there are 5 appearances, by which time he has acknowledged that one of the issues is control of heresy. Then he turns to the distinction, incredibly difficult to make, between 'best books' and 'bad books' (*CPW* 2: 512). The more frequently the word 'book' appears, the more hopeless the task, not only of discrimination, but of stemming the flood. It is ridiculous to seek to prevent immorality (Milton's word is 'sin') by removing its cause, 'for besides that it is a huge heap increasing under the very act of diminishing, though some part of it may for a time be withdrawn from some persons, it cannot from all, in such a universal thing as books are' (527). This would mean forbidding everything, supervising every experience in modern life, 'for what ever thing we hear or see, sitting, walking, traveling, or conversing may be fitly call'd our book, and is of the same effect as writings are' (528). Plus the licensers will have to go back and repeal or proscribe 'all scandalous and unlicenc't books already printed and divulged' (528), which even to list would be prohibitively expensive of labor. And what about those heretical sects 'refusing books as a hindrance, and preserving their doctrine unmixt for many ages, only by unwritt'n traditions' (529)? We are now in the land of the crazies. In showing the absurdity of the premises on which the Order is based, Milton spares a word of sympathy for the wretched licenser enforced to read what he has not chosen, 'and in a hand scars legible, whereof three pages would not down at any time in the fairest Print' (520). Pre-publication censorship cannot possibly work, especially given the shortage of qualified censors.

While leaning towards the ludicrous, Milton's argument has a strong practical basis. Look, he writes: 'Do we not see... weekly that continu'd Court-libell against the Parlament and City, Printed, as the wet sheets can witnes, and dispers't among us, for all that licensing can doe?' You can almost see him

testing the ink with a finger. Even more telling, both of the
actual workings of the book trade and of Milton's personal
involvement in it, is the passage in which he deals with the
problem of authorial alterations after copy has been delivered:

> And what if the author shall be one so copious of fancie,
> as to have many things well worth the adding, come into
> his mind after licensing, while the book is yet under the
> Presse, which not seldom happ'ns to the best and dili-
> gentest writers; and that perhaps a dozen times in one
> book. The Printer dares not go beyond his licenc't copy;
> so often then must the author trudge to his leav-giver,
> that those his new insertions may be viewd; and many a
> jaunt will be made, ere that licencer, for it must be the
> same man, can either be found, or found at leisure; mean
> while either the Presse must stand still, which is no small
> damage, or the author loose his accuratest thought, &
> send the book forth wors then he had made it, which to
> a diligent writer is the greatest melancholy and vex-
> ation.   (*CPW* 2: 532)

We have met this worthy man to whom it 'not seldom happ'ns'
to have afterthoughts in the *Doctrine and Discipline of Divorce*.
And it is not by coincidence, therefore, that *Areopagitica* is
introduced to its primary audience with a variant of the authorial peekaboo, the 'he who' strategy that connected the author of
the church-reform pamphlets to the author of the divorce
pamphlets: 'For he who freely magnifies what hath been nobly
done, and fears not to declare as freely what might be done
better, gives ye the best cov'nant of his fidelity' (*CPW* 2: 488).

To the point where Milton gives us a mini-anecdote of his own authorial frustrations at the hands of a licenser, *Areopagitica*, then, belongs not to the history of liberal thought but to the material history of the book, of which the survey of censorship up to and including this moment is a not inconsiderable contribution. The turning point is, I think, Milton's second quotation from Sir Francis Bacon's *Wise and Moderate Discourse concerning Church-Affaires*, as first published in 1640. The first quotation turns on 'authoriz'd books' (*CPW* 2: 534), the second on 'a certain spark of truth that flies up in the faces of them who seeke to tread it out' (542). From this moment Milton turns his attention to the concept of Truth, who now appears as a female person. She has a wicked 'stepdame', the parliamentary Order, who would keep her in the dungeon. Then she is 'the virgin Truth', undoubtedly related to Spenser's Una in the first book of *The Faerie Queene*, but now with martyrdom to her credit. She 'came once into the world with her divine Master', but after the primitive age of the Church 'then strait arose a wicked race of deceivers, who ... took the virgin Truth, hewd her lovely form into a thousand peeces, and scatter'd them to the four winds' (549). This revision of the myth of Osiris, in which the 'sad friends of Truth, such as durst appear' have been going up and down the world gathering up the fragments and attempting to piece them together, starts as a tragedy, though a happy ending is posited. 'We have not yet found them all, Lords and Commons, nor ever shall doe, till her Masters second comming,' wrote Milton in a brilliant intuition that this was his strongest and most positive argument for the unfettering of the press. Truth was a work in progress. Not only the Reformation, but Revelation itself, were incomplete and fragmentary. Finally, though inconsistently, the virgin Truth becomes a warrior maiden, not a Una but a Britomart, who is quite capable of taking care of herself:

> And though all the windes of doctrin were let loose to play upon the earth, so Truth be in the field, we do injuriously by licencing and prohibiting to misdoubt her strength. Let her and Falshood grapple; who ever knew Truth put to the wors, in a free and open encounter.... For who knows not that Truth is strong next to the Almighty;... give her but room, & do not bind her when she sleeps, for then she speaks not true, as the old Proteus did, who spake oracles only when he was caught & bound, but then rather she turns herself into all shapes except her own, and perhaps tunes her voice according to the times. (561–63)

We have now at least four different myths in play, which can be puzzling if one thinks logically; however, these are the passages that warm the literary heart. And if Milton's imagination were sparked by Bacon's trope of a fire that cannot be trodden out, we know that he was echoing William Walwyn's *Compassionate Samaritane* when he formulated his Amazonian fantasy.

To look carefully at Milton's words in this tract, then, is to get closer to his original intention and also his working methods. By the end, we can see that something miraculous has happened. Books, those material objects, have become an immaterial idea; and Truth, the abstraction, has acquired a physical body, all the more material for having been torn in pieces.

Readie & Easie Way

LIBERTY. 'Not the word only, but the thing itself.' The word in question, in this crucial phrase from both versions of Milton's *Readie & Easie Way to Establish a Free Commonwealth*, was 'liberty'. More importantly, it was the verbal hinge between two originally separate ideas: civil liberty, which for Milton now meant a federalized republic, or almost anything other than a return to monarchy; and spiritual liberty, or freedom of conscience, free from the legislated uniformity of belief which, he could see, a restored monarchy would entail. But the hinge was not only verbal. The originality of the *Readie & Easie Way* was in arguing, and in clarifying the argument by strenuous verbal revision, that the two kinds of liberty were not just analogous but structurally, causally, essentially interdependent. You could not hope for freedom of conscience under a king (or a dictator), because the right to determine the tenets of one's own belief solely by reading the Scriptures led directly to political radicalism: 'For they hear the Gospel speaking much of libertie, a word which monarchie and her bishops both fear and hate; but a free Commonwealth both favours and promotes; and not the word only, but the thing itself.'

Unlike *Areopagitica*, the *Readie & Easie Way* is not one of the best known or most admired of Milton's political pamphlets. There are several reasons for this. The greatest disincentive, probably, is the complicated process of revision the text went through between its first and its second editions, hereafter designated *REW 1* and *2*. The first version may have been jump started when General Monck began his march down from Scotland on February 4, 1660, and certainly before February 22, when the Rump Parliament, led by the previously secluded members, agreed to a new election, which was what Monck wanted. The second edition must have been composed after the dissolution of the old parliament on March 16 and probably preceded March 27, the date of the arrest of Livewell Chapman, the bookseller for the first edition, for publishing 'seditious and treasonable books'. The much shorter *REW1* might therefore have taken Milton about two weeks to write. For *REW2* he had only about ten days, for an infinitely more complex task (*CPW* 7: 340–45). Everything about it, including its date of publication, is a mystery. The volume identified neither publisher nor printer, and there are only three extant copies, suggesting both fugitive printing and/or immediate suppression, possibly by Milton himself.

Not only did the pamphlet almost double in length; it appears that every sentence was reassessed. The insertions were not only in large separate chunks but also in sentences carefully tucked in so that the seams did not show, and even articles and prepositions were adjusted to produce exactly the right effect. It needs hardly be said that this would have been a challenge for a sighted man, however over-excited; but Milton was by now completely blind. He must have had a willing and patient accomplice—a better word than amanuensis in this instance— and we might guess that either Edward Phillips or Marchamont Nedham (or both) were involved. Although Milton's revisions were meticulously noted by Robert Ayers, the editor of both editions for the Yale *Complete Prose*, comparing the two versions, as they exist separately in the Yale and side by side in the

Oxford editions, is a form of drudgery few would embrace; certainly not those scholars, primarily intellectual historians, whose interest in the word 'liberty' is on the grand scale.

A second reason for the neglect of *Readie & Easie Way* amounts to an aversion to its central proposal—that the only system of government to which England could now safely turn would be that of a unicameral parliament, and one not subject to the vagaries of elections. Milton proposed a perpetually sitting senate, a 'Grand Councel', whose most obvious model was the Venetian Senate, its members only replaceable on their death, or indictment of a crime. Thus the vaunted balance of powers in the English constitution was to be replaced by the rule of an oligarchy of 'chosen Patriots' (*REW2*, p. 443). In the second edition, having heard complaints that 'long continuance of power may corrupt sincerest men' (*REW2*, pp. 434–35), Milton leaned a little closer to James Harrington's theory of 'partial rotation', by suggesting that a third of the Senate could be replaced by elections, that third to be identified by their seniority (*REW2*, pp. 434–35). Our instinctive rejection of such a system ought to be slightly qualified, however, by Milton's intention that the business of such a Senate should be foreign policy, national finance, the laws governing commerce, and national security. For everything else, government would be decentralized. Each county would become 'a little common-wealth' (*REW1*, p. 383), to deal with 'all things of civil government between man and man. So they shall have justice in thir own hands'. Unfortunately this practical idea—of regional government for regional affairs—was also pushed in the direction of elitism by Milton's assumption that the local administration of justice would naturally devolve upon 'the nobilitie and chief gentry'. Thus Milton laid himself open, in what was almost his last foray into politics, to the charge of being antidemocratic.

It is fair to say that 'liberty' is the primary keyword of the *Readie & Easie Way*. In the second edition it appears 43 times, liberally buttressed, of course, by 'freedom', 'freely', and 'free', the latter not least when attached, as in Milton's title, to 'Commonwealth', as *that* word's proper definition. A 'free Commonwealth' is mentioned, hoped for, or despaired of no less than 15 times. This choric (or vatic) repetition has still greater effect in the original print, where the phrase can be seen to dominate the tiny pages. By comparison, the *Tenure of Kings and Magistrates*, where Milton had first worked out his theory of government, used 'liberty' only 13 times. Its verbal hammers were liberty's opposite, 'Tyrant' and 'tyranny'.

In the year of Milton's quatercentenary (2008) a conference was held on 'Civil and Religious Liberty' at Yale University, one of whose goals was to track the evolution of those ideas in seventeenth- and eighteenth-century England. In a paper entitled 'Milton and Liberty', Blair Worden, a historian preeminent for spanning the literary/historical divide, cited Milton's *Considerations touching the likeliest means to remove hirelings out of the church* (1659) as the first occasion on which civil and religious liberty were 'bracketed' in print by an author we can name. 'Bracketed' chimes with my own earlier statement that in the *Readie & Easie Way* the word 'liberty' functions as a verbal hinge between what are more often thought of as separate ideals, civil rights and freedom of conscience. Worden qualified his assertion of an originary moment by the disclaimer 'As far as I know'. Yet, as far as I myself know, Milton was thinking of Sir Henry Vane's definition of the Good Old Cause in *A Healing Question Propounded*, which was first published in 1656. This anti-Cromwellian manifesto asserted that the Cause had two parts: 'to restore to this [nation] their just natural Rights in civil things, and true freedome in matters of conscience' (p. 3). This pairing was not just a weak 'and': Vane referred to his two freedoms, which he thought abrogated under the Protectorate, as two 'Branches' of the same tree. One of his recommendations for reform was the establishment of a standing council. Vane's pamphlet was republished by Thomas Brewster, its original sponsor, under the date 1660, though probably late in 1659. It looks as though Milton came across it half way through *REW1*, since on p. 14 of the original pamphlet he seems to make a new start: 'The whole freedom of man consists either in spiritual or civil liberty.' But where Vane had started with civil liberty, Milton starts with spiritual liberty, and then, on p. 16, turns to 'the other part of our freedom [which] consists in the civil rights and advanc'ments of every person according to his merit'. This, Milton's first brief description of a federal system, is a different approach to civil liberty from Vane's; but it is surely significant that he rounds it off by remarking, 'What I have spoken, is the language of the good old cause' (*CPW* 7: 387). In the second edition, Milton retained the binary structure of liberty, and in one instance even changed 'liberty' to 'liberty and religion', a small change with a huge import, as noted by Ayers (*CPW* 7: 421).

Milton's probable debt to Vane had already been indicated by Austin Woolrych (7: 19–20) as part of his magnificent introduction to that volume of the Yale Prose that deals with the turbulent period between the death of Oliver Cromwell and the actual decision to recall Charles II. Woolrych also stressed the contributions of Henry Stubbe, a client of Vane, who in October 1659 recommended the creation of a '*Select Senate*, or Conservators of the liberties of England', who like Milton's would serve for life, though this guarantee of stability was to be combined with biennially elected parliaments (*CPW* 7: 127–28). In the ferment of the moment, every system of government imaginable was proffered to the public in print, and it is only because we know Milton's proposal better (because it is Milton's) that its constitutional inadequacy strikes us so hard. But what I am more concerned with than the proposal, or its considerable modifications in the second edition, is the binary structure of liberty that Milton inherited from Vane, the conceptual leap that Worden called 'bracketing' and I call a 'hinge'. In both versions of the *Readie & Easie Way*, however, Milton went beyond Vane in explaining how spiritual liberty would be dependent for its survival on the system of government eventually chosen. We can see this most clearly in the second edition.

In fact the sentence quoted at the beginning of this section, with its brilliant center, 'not the word only, but the thing itself', acquires in the second edition a hinge-like structure of its own. Let us see precisely how the revision works, by superimposing the second edition on the first. In what follows, what survives of *REW1* is represented by standard type, what was deleted by italics, and what was added by bold:

> The whole freedom of man consists either in spiritual or
> civil libertie. As for spiritual, who can be at rest, who can

enjoy anything in this world with contentment, who hath
not libertie to serve God and save his own soul, according
to the best light which God hath planted in him to that
purpose, by the reading of his reveal'd will and the guidance of his holy spirit? That this is best pleasing to God, and
that the whole Protestant Church allows no supream judge
or rule in matters of religion, but the scriptures, and these
to be interpreted by the scriptures themselves, which ne-
cessarily infers liberty of conscience, {*hath bin heretofore
prov'd at large in other treatises*}, [**I have heretofore prov'd
at large in another treatise**] and might yet further by the
publick declarations, confessions, and admonitions of
whole Churches and States, obvious in all historie, since
the Reformation. {*He who cannot be content with this
libertie to himself, but seeks violently to impose what he
will have to be the only religion, upon other men's consciences, let him know, bears a minde not only unchristian
and irreligious, but inhuman also and barbarous. And in
my judgment civil States would do much better, and remove
the cause of much hindrance and disturbance in publick
affairs, much ambition, much hypocrisie and contention
among the people, if they would not meddle at all with
Ecclesiastical matters, which are both of a quite different
nature from their cognizance, and have thir proper laws
fully and completely with such coercive power as belongs to
them ordaind by Christ himself and his apostles. If ther were
no medling with Church matters in State counsels, there
would not be such faction in chusing members of Parlament,
while every one strives to chuse him whom he takes to be of*

his religion; and everie faction hath the plea of Gods cause.
Ambitious leaders of armies would then have no hypocrit-
ical pretences so ready at hand to contest with Parlaments,
yea to dissolve them and make way to thir own tyrannical
designs; in sum, I verily suppose ther would be then no more
pretending to a fifth monarchie of the saints; but much peace
amd tranquillitie would follow; as the United Netherlands
have found by experience; who while they persecuted the
Arminians, were in much disquiet among themselves, and
in danger to have broke asunder into a civil war; since they
have left off persecuting, they have livd in much more
concord and prosperitie And I have heard from Polanders
themselves, that they never enjoid more peace, then when
religion was most at libertie among them; that then first
began thir troubles, when that king by instigation of the
Jesuites began to force the Cossaks in matters of religion.}
This libertie of conscience, which above all other things
ought to be to all men dearest and most precious, no
government more inclinable not only to favour but to
protect, then a free Commonwealth; as being most mag-
nanimous, most fearless and confident of its own fair
proceedings. Wheras kingship, though looking big, yet
indeed most pusillanimous, full of fears, full of jealousies,
startl'd at everie umbrage, as it hath bin observd of old to
have ever suspected most and mistrusted them who were
in most esteem for virtue and generositie of minde, so it is
now known to have most in doubt and suspicion them
who are most reputed to be religious. Q. Elizabeth, though
her self accounted so good a Protestant, so moderate, so

confident of her subjects love, would never give way so
much as to Presbyterian reformation in this land, though
once and again besought, as Cambden relates, but impri-
sond and persecuted the verie proposers therof, alleaging it
as her minde and maxim unalterable, that such reformation would diminish regal authoritie. What libertie of
conscience can we then expect {*from*} [**of**] others far
worse principl'd from the cradle, traind up and governd
by Popish and Spanish counsels, and on such depending
hitherto for subsistence? [**Especially what can this last
Parlament expect, who having reviv'd lately and publishd
the covnant, have reingag'd themselves, never to readmit
Episcopacie; which no son of Charls returning, but will
most certainly bring back with him, if he regard the last
and strictest charge of his father,** *to persevere in not the
doctrin only, but government of the church of England; not to
neglect the speedie and effectual suppressing of errors and
schisms* [italics original, as indicating a quotation from
Eikon Basilike] **among which he accounted Presbyterie
one of the chief: or if not withstanding that charge of his
father, he submit to the covnant, how will he keep faith to
us with disobedience to him; or regard that faith given,
which must be founded on the breach of that last and
solemnest paternal charge, and the reluctance, I may say
the antipathie which is in all kings against Presbyterian
and Independent discipline?**] For they hear the Gospel
speaking much of libertie, a word which monarchie and
her bishops both fear and hate; but a free Commonwealth
both favours and promotes; and not the word only, but the

thing itself. [But let our governors beware in time, least thir hard measure to libertie of conscience be found the rock wheron they shipwrack themselves as others have now don before them in the cours wherein God was directing thir steerage to a free Commonwealth, and the abandoning of all those whom they call *sectaries*, for the detected falshood and ambition of som, be a willful rejection of thir own chief strength and interest in the freedom of all Protestant religion, under what abusive name soever calumniated.]

Of this revision, which Woolrych calls Milton's 'largest single excision', there has been some discussion as to its motives, none to my mind very convincing (*CPW* 7: 212–13). Perhaps Milton, who had now decided General Monck was the equivalent of the Roman dictator Sulla, became wary of the reference to 'ambitious leaders of armies', which Ayers believed referred back to Cromwell (*CPW* 7: 380), but which had now become a two-edged sword. One of its oddities is that the deleted passage began with that phrase hitherto a surrogate for Milton himself: '*He who*', but which now excoriates the person who thinks like this as 'not only unchristian and irreligious, but inhuman also and barbarous'. Once the passage was excised, this stylistic and psychological inconsistency vanished. Much less has been said of what was added, which amounts to almost exactly the same number of words as were removed. Nothing has been said about the way the hinge sentence has been carefully bled into the new material as if it belonged exclusively to it. It seems to me that Milton decided to remove the arguments from the history of toleration in other countries, the Dutch Republic and Poland, in order to focus all his logical force on the connection between intolerance and *monarchy*. He retained Queen Elizabeth, whose behavior towards the Presbyterians he had learned of from Camden's *Annales*, and hooked onto her the 'son of Charls returning' as one of the hereditary kings whose antipathy to Presbyterians and Independents, as themselves antipathetical to hierarchy, is inherent in their view of royal power. The younger Charles, moreover, has been sworn by his father in *Eikon Basilike* to restore the Church of England in its original form. The revised passage, therefore, has a tighter, more national focus. And the added warning to 'our governors', presumably Monck and those in charge of the electoral process, also looks backward to the 'others' in the previous regimes, both Charles I and Cromwell, who have shipwrecked on the rock of intolerance. It would have been much easier to excise the entire block of material than to interleave the old with the new in this way.

Thus Milton was not the first to tie religious and civil liberty together, but he tied them tighter, and, we might say, more politically, than did Vane. Elsewhere in his revisions, where the changes are not in blocks but in phrases, it is clear that he knew that every word would matter. And now I want to argue something surprising: that by the time he had finished revising the *Readie & Easie Way* it was not, in its language, quite as anti-democratic as we have thought. The peroration still draws back in horror from 'a misguided and abus'd multitude' (p. 463), but even here Milton substituted 'a' for the 'the' of the original, which makes the anticipated defection less nation-wide.

THE PEOPLE. Another word, or phrase, easier to overlook than the high-minded 'liberty' is 'people', or, more to the ideological point, 'the people'. This deceptively simple phrase, derived of course from Latin *populus*, and flagged as noble in the Latin title of both Milton's *Defenses* of the English people, could also carry the condescending sense of 'multitude', which by the time of Raymond Williams had been clarified by the introduction of 'masses' as a substitute. In the *Tenure of Kings and Magistrates* Milton had used 'the people' positively, and frequently enough to be challenged by Salmasius in *Defensio Regia*, where a definition was demanded. To which Milton replied in the *First Defense*:

> 'It behooves us English to tell you', you say, 'what we mean by the word People'.... This you suppose you know, that by the word people we mean the common people only, because 'we have abolished the House of Lords'. And yet this is the very thing that shows that under the word people we comprehend all our citizens of what order and degree soever; in that we have a single supreme Commons' House only, in which the lords also have by law the right to vote as a part of the people.   (*CE* 7: 391)

And in the next paragraph he accepts the Salmasian view of the common people as 'ventosius, vanius, levius, mobilius', but explains that in *his* use of the term *populus* means not the *plebs* but the middle sort, 'amongst whom the wisest men and most skilful in affairs are generally found' (*CE* 7: 392–93).

If frequency of usage may indicate a keyword, then increased frequency of usage should confirm such a hypothesis. But numbers alone will not tell us what we need. In *REW1* Milton used 'the

People' 27 times. In *REW2* he used it 35 times. But in *REW1* several of those appearances had been disparaging, ('bad principles and fals apprehensions among too many of the people', p. 355; 'an abject people', p. 361; 'that people must needs be madd or strangely infatuated', p. 361; 'the impatient or disaffected people', p. 365; 'hypocrisie and contention among the people', p. 380; 'if the people be so affected, as to prostitute religion and libertie', p. 385). In *REW2*, while the disparaging phrases were not removed, the added ones leaned in the direction of political idealism: 'They [the Long Parliament] knew the people of England to be a free people', p. 411; 'the best affected also and best principl'd of the people', p. 414; 'the majesty of a free people', p. 428; 'the people might have soon bin satisfi'd and delighted with the decent order', p. 430; 'inspectors deputed for satisfaction of the people', p. 433; 'To make the people fittest to chuse ... to teach the people faith not without virtue ... the people then will have thir several ordinarie assemblies', p. 443; and, most interestingly, as part of the concession to partial rotation of the senators, 'that it be at those times in the peoples choice, whether they will change them, or renew thir power, as they shall finde cause', p. 461.

DEMOCRACY. One must conclude from this process that Milton had by now two competing ideas of what he meant by 'the people', one frustratedly anti-populist, the other the central concept he had formulated in the *Tenure of Kings and Magistrates*. This position was as close to imagining democracy as Milton could have been expected to reach, and we can see him reaching back for it in both versions of the *Readie & Easie Way*, though more clearly in *REW2*. To use the word 'democracy' here is not anachronistic (although Sumner's translation of the *First Defense* often uses it misleadingly for 'popular government'), for in *REW* Milton used the term himself. We should dwell on this for a moment, because it is more than a quibble. In *Of Reformation* he was still a monarchist, and observed that there is nothing 'more baneful to *Monarchy* then a Popular Commotion, for the dissolution of Monarchy slides aptest into a *Democraty*' (*CPW* 1: 592), a prospect that here Milton is certainly not recommending. In *Areopagitica* he admires Isocrates, 'who from his private house wrote that discourse to the Parlament of Athens, that perswades them to change the forme of *Democraty* which was then establisht' (*CPW* 2: 489), that is, by recommending it become *less* democratic. By the time Milton wrote the *Readie & Easie Way*, of course, the distinction he had made in the *First Defense* had broken down, along with the structure of the House of Commons. In fact, the *Way* was preceded by the unpublished *Letter to a Friend*, written in October 1659, by which time Milton's thoughts on democracy were blowing in the wind. In the crisis spilling from Oliver Cromwell's death, all constitutional possibilities were back on the table: 'Whether the civill government be an annuall **democracy** or a perpetual Aristocracy', Milton wrote, perhaps to John Bradshaw, then on his death bed, 'is too nice a consideracion for the extremities wherein wee are' (*CPW* 7: 331):

> That it be not an Oligarchy or the faction of a few, may be easily prevented by the numbers of their own chusing... Full liberty of conscience, & the abjuracion of Monarchy propos'd: & the well ordered committies of

> their faithfullest adherents in every county may give this
> government the resemblance & effects of a perfect
> **democracie**.   (7: 331)

By 'annual democracy' he presumably meant a House of Commons reelected yearly. Six months later he had clarified his own
thinking, and settled, if not for a 'perpetual Aristocracy', at least
a perpetual Senate of the wiser sort.

Democracy does not appear at all in the first edition of *REW*.
For the second edition, however, Milton introduced it in two of
his added passages—which seem diametrically to contradict each
other. First, at least in the order of the pamphlet we now have, he
added a gloss on his own citation of Proverbs 6: 6–8, Solomon's
advice to look to the kingless ants for a successful polity:

> neither are these diligent creatures hence concluded to
> live in lawless anarchie, or that commended, but are set
> the examples to imprudent and ungoverned men, of a
> frugal and self-governing *democratie* or Commonwealth;
> safer and more thriving in the joint providence and
> counsel of many industrious equals, then under the sin-
> gle domination of one imperious Lord.   (*CPW* 7: 427)

And then, seeking to reject the argument that previous models of
perpetual senates had constitutional counterbalances, as the Are-
opagus in Athens or the tribunate in Rome, he asserted that 'these
remedies either little availd the people, or brought them to such a
licentious and unbridl'd *democratie*, as in fine ruind themselves with
their own excessive power' (7: 438). This anti-Machiavellian account
of the Roman tribunate is then cursorily linked to the moment when

Marius, alarmed by the extremist democratic measures executed by the tribunes of his day, turned against them, which led to the first Roman civil war and the military dictatorship of Sulla. One might say that the second, hostile invocation of 'democracy' trumps the first, or that history trumps natural science; except that the title page of *REW2* uses that same moment in Roman history to rebalance both versions. When Milton chose not just to cite but to alter Juvenal's position, 'et nos | consilium dedimus Sullae', by adding 'demus populo nunc' ('We have advised Sulla, now we advise the people'), he both alluded to the failure of his own attempts to influence General Monck, in *REW1*, and redefined his audience and his position with extreme verbal sophistication.

Of True Religion, Haeresie, Schism, Toleration and what best means may be us'd against the growth of POPERY

In 1673, after he had arranged for the re-publication of his collected poems and his grammar and logic textbooks, Milton suddenly reentered the field of printed polemic, and published the tract whose verbose title is displayed above. The title strings together words (one is a phrase) that had recently become keywords in the sense used by Raymond Williams: that is, words on everyone's lips, used in debates in the House of Commons, and in the text of a recent royal proclamation. The context was the struggle between the Anglicans in the Commons, who insisted on asserting the Act of Uniformity and on backing it up with civil penalties, and Charles II, who had now made two attempts to modify the Act in favor both of Protestant Dissenters and Roman Catholics, most recently in his

1672 Declaration of Indulgence, which the Commons had just forced him to withdraw. '*True religion*' echoed the proclamation of March 13, as did '*the growth of Popery*', a shocking locution in the king's mouth. Anti-Catholic prejudice, which in 1673 had been reexcited by the remarriage of James, duke of York, to the Catholic duchess of Modena, depended on the erroneous belief that Roman Catholics were increasing in number in England but also on proof of their influence at court. '*Schism*' had of course been a term deployed by the Presbyterians in the early 1640s, and raised to the level of a keyword by John Hales. Hales's influential little tract, *Concerning Schisme and Schismatiques* (1642), had been recently resurrected by Andrew Marvell in the *Rehearsal Transpros'd*, Marvell's first defense of the king's abortive attempts at indulgence 'for tender consciences'. Milton himself had used it as a keyword in the *Reason of Church Government*, where in Book 1, Chapter 6, he deployed 'schism' and its derivatives no less than 44 times, to make mock of the arguments of the bishops against permitting disagreement. '*Heresy*' is the odd man out, about which more below. And finally '*Toleration*', the word that Milton had only used in *Areopagitica* because he was citing Lord Brooke, was now the talk of the town. It had appeared in the titles of a number of Restoration pamphlets, such as John Owen's *Indulgence and Toleration Considered* (1667), or Thomas Tomkins's *The Inconveniencies of Toleration* (1667), or William Assheton's *Toleration disapprov'd and condemn'd* (1670, 1671), or Sir Roger L'Estrange's many times published *Toleration discuss'd*, one edition of which appeared in 1673. At least in print the conformists outnumbered the toleration-ists. In this his last tract, Milton himself deployed 'toleration' or its variants no less than 12 times. But I am sorry to say that his use of the term fell on *both* sides of the divide.

Milton, who had notoriously exempted Roman Catholicism from the press freedom espoused in *Areopagitica*, now made matters worse. His position was intellectually untenable. To put it bluntly, he reaffirmed the need for freedom of inquiry, freedom of speech and of the press for all Protestants, and denied it to Roman Catholics. This meant tolerating Lutherans, strict Calvinists, Anabaptists, Arians, Socinians, and Arminians as merely mistaken in one or other point of doctrine, but refusing toleration to Catholics. Why? Because international Catholicism was a political threat, the position of the Whig opposition in parliament; but also because even the private practice of the Roman Catholic religion involved idolatry. This claim is buttressed by a bizarre quotation from Ezekiel that involves a hole in the wall, digging, and things done in the dark.

The one word in Milton's title that was not at that time noticeably a keyword, but which he here elevated to that status, is *Heresy*. We can understand its presence better if we suspect that it was just about now, 1673, that Milton wrote the Epistle to his *De Doctrina Christiana*, in which he declared his willingness to make that heretical document public, in the interests of free discussion and the search after truth. Without this freedom, he wrote, 'we are still enslaved, not, as once, by the Law of God, but, what is vilest of all, by human law, or rather to be more exact, an inhuman tyranny':

There are some irrational bigots who, by a perversion of justice, condemn anything they consider inconsistent with conventional beliefs and give it an invidious title—'heretic' or 'heresy'—without consulting the evidence of the Bible upon this point. To their way of thinking, by branding anyone out of hand with this hateful name, they silence him with one word and need take no further trouble . . . I retort that, in apostolic times, before the New Testament was written, the word heresy, whenever it was used as an accusation, was applied only to something which contradicted the teaching of the apostles as it passed from mouth to mouth . . . On the same grounds I hold that, since the compilation of the New Testament, nothing can correctly be called heresy unless it contradicts that. For my own part, I devote my attention to the Holy Scriptures alone.

(*CPW* 6: 123–24)

This bold statement explains why Milton was willing, in *Of True Religion*, to offer toleration to Arians, Socinian, and Arminians, all of whose positions he partially adopted in the *De Doctrina*.

Words Apart: Quarantining the Keywords

The following argument began as a response to an international conference entitled *Milton: Rights and Liberties*, which took for granted that 'right' and 'liberty' were political keywords for Milton, and encouraged us to find them everywhere in his work. If we consider frequency of use as a key to mental habits, however, it is interesting to see that the tract that uses 'liberty' most often is *Tetrachordon*, suggesting that Milton arrived at his concepts of political liberty by way of the divorce pamphlets, or, as he stated disingenuously in the *Second Defense*, by way of thinking about civil liberty. *Tetrachordon* has 28 appearances of liberty, whereas *Areopagitica* has only half as many.

In the *Tenure of Kings and Magistrates*, certainly, both *liberty* and *right(s)* are used as poles of his argument, and we can see that Milton has come to full political consciousness. He was perhaps influenced by Henry Parker's *Answer* to Charles I's answer to the Nineteen Propositions put forward by the Long Parliament to curb the royal prerogative; but Parker only insisted on the rights of parliament, not of the people at large. We know that Milton read John Sadleir's *Rights of the Kingdom*, which had just appeared in 1649 when he was attacking *Eikon Basilike*, because he refers specifically to it (*CPW* 3: 399). In the *Tenure* Milton worked primarily within the vocabulary of tyrannomachia, as derived from such figures as Buchanan and the *Vindiciae contra Tyrannos*, noted in his Commonplace Book, where his primary keyword is *Tyrant*, with a section of its own. There is also a section on *Liberty*, which ends with a citation on tyrants from Guicciardini. But when he came to write the *Tenure* Milton had enlarged his thinking. Tyrannomachia alone is too narrow for his new purpose. He now drew on both abstract political theory and English constitutional history, producing a somewhat mongrel argument. In terms of abstract political theory, Milton adduced the Aristotelian version of the state of nature, but now modified by Christian notions of the Fall. 'All men naturally were borne free', and remained so 'Till from the root of Adams transgression, falling among themselves to doe wrong and violence', they had, in Hobbesian fashion, to contract out for a governor, in the interests of 'self-defence and preservation'. 'It follows', wrote Milton, in a move that Hobbes would specifically reject, 'that since the King or Magistrate holds his autoritie of the people,...then may the people as oft as they shall judge it for the best, either choose him or reject him, retaine him or depose him though no Tyrant, meerly by the *liberty* and *right* of free born Men, to be govern'd as seems to them best' (p. 206). Needless to say, the state of nature is one of which we have no records.

In terms of English constitutional history, however, where records do exist, the story comes out pretty much the same:

> Whence doubtless our Ancestors who were not ignorant with what *rights* either Nature or ancient Constitution had endowd them,...thought it no way illegal to depose and put to death tyrannous Kings. Insomuch that the Parlament drew up a charge against Richard the second, and the Commons requested to have judgement de-cree'd against him, that the realme might not bee endan-gered.... But far before these days, Gildas, the most ancient of all our Historians, speaking of those times wherein the Roman Empire quitted and relinquished what *right* they had by Conquest to this Iland, and resign'd it all into the peoples hands, testifies that the people thus reinvested with thir own original *right*,... both elected them Kings, whom they thought best... and by the same *right*, when they apprehended cause, usually depos'd and put them to death.   (p. 221)

These statements are explicitly designed to override the use of the term 'right' to designate a monarch's legal hold over his territories, whether hereditary or by conquest, the sense in which 'right' appears frequently in the regicide pamphlets, almost as frequently as its challenger. Thus Milton acknowledges, if indirectly, that rights talk is always labile, unstable, and two-sided.

It would be tedious to set out in any kind of detail the manner in which Milton took these premises and elaborated them in *Defensio pro Populo Anglicano*. But there is one passage in the *First Defense* that we should listen to again. Milton is refuting the claim by Salmasius, based on Jeremiah 27: 7, that God gave many kingdoms over into servitude under Nebuchadnezzar. But he denies that this can be extrapolated into showing that he gave the English people over for a moment ('ad semihorulam') into servitude under Charles Stuart:

> That God allowed this I would not deny, but I have never heard that he gave them. Or if God be said to give a people into slavery whenever a tyrant prevails over the people, why ought he not as well be said to set them free whenever the people prevail over a tyrant? Shall the tyrant credit and owe his tyranny to God, and not we our liberty?   (*CE* 7: 180–81)

By the time Milton gets to the *Readie & Easie Way*, second edition, *liberty*, as we have seen, has become dominant. To mark the change in tone, Milton added a new introduction in which he begs for 'a little Shroving-time...wherin to...take our leaves of Libertie', where the keyword is dignified by capitalization. It is richly supported, as in the title, by the words 'free' and 'Commonwealth', usually sutured together to indicate a new political idea. *Right(s)*, on the other hand, virtually disappears, at least in its populist sense. If you call the king back, however, Milton warns, that *other* sense of *right* will reestablish itself:

> For it is only the king's right, he will say, to call a parlament; and...what will thir business then be and the chief expence of thir time, but an endless tugging between petition of right and royal prerogative.
>
> (*CPW* 7: 446)

And then comes the moment of betrayal. In response to the appeal to majoritarianism, Milton declared: 'This greatest part have both in reason and the trial of just battel, lost the right of their election what the government shall be: of them who have not lost that right, whether they for kingship be the greater number, who can certainly determin' (7: 455). Faced with opinion polls that indicated most of the nation wanted monarchy back, Milton calmly deprived them of any vote on the matter; and as to the few good men who had kept true to the republican cause, their opinion can probably not be canvassed.

I referred above to the occasion for the drafting of this argument, the international conference entitled 'Milton: Rights and Liberties', that took place in 2005. Such an occasion requires one to search for these terms or concepts wherever one can, or wherever one can't. In the course of writing my response, I came to realize, unwillingly, that, whereas 'rights' and 'liberties' are central to the texts of Milton's life as a pamphleteer, they are carefully *excluded* from, or carefully disenabled, in his poetry. Having liberally peppered his prose with the keywords of political activism, when Milton turned or turned back to poetry he put those words under strong advisement.

Few would disagree that, today, the main problem with the three great poems is how we are to align them with the polemical prose. The strategies we use to bend them into our desired shape are many. In this case, my 'we' is the sign of complicity, because I have been one of the worst offenders. We focus on the fragments of *Paradise Lost* that feed our wishes, from the opening allusion to ancient liberty in the prefatory note on blank verse, to the attack by Adam on Nimrod as the first king and the first tyrant, which is also a refutation of Filmer. We extract the crumb of hope inserted into the account of the creation of the insects, 'the parsimonious emmet... Pattern of just equality perhaps | Hereafter' (*PL* 7: 485–88, forgetting its difference from the unqualified praise of the commonwealth of ants in *Readie & Easie Way*, who are 'safer and more thriving in the joint providence of many industrious equals, then under the single domination of one imperious Lord' (*CPW* 7: 427). We argue that the huge gap between the language of the *Readie & Easie Way* and *Paradise Lost* on the subject of monarchy as an institution is ontologically intelligible because the monarch in the latter is God, not Charles II. We conceive of the poem as a new Exodus, with Milton as a new Moses, leading the defeated republicans for nearly forty years 'Through the wild desert, not the readiest way' (*PL* 12: 216), overlooking this joke at the *Way's* expense. And most of all, we turn to Milton's reassurance to his readers at the opening of Book 7, that he is 'unchanged | To hoarse or mute, though fall'n on evil days' (*PL* 7: 24–25). We, and especially myself, have looked to this last instance as the sign that *Paradise Lost must* have encoded the resistance that it manifestly refuses, or refuses manifestly, to articulate.

But I think we need to be honest about the vocabulary of *Paradise Lost*. Here the word 'liberty' appears a mere 12 times (as compared to the 43 occurrences in *REW*2.) Nine of these are demonic—that is to say, they are spoken by the fallen angels—and three are direct parodies of the argument of the *Way*. Thus Mammon sets out a proposal for entrepreneurial freedom, 'Free, and to none accountable, preferring | Hard liberty before the easy yoke | Of servile pomp' (*PL* 2: 256). In the *Way* Milton anticipates the restoration of monarchy as leading to 'the perpetual bowings and cringing of an abject people, on either side deifying and adoring him' (*CPW* 7: 427). In *Paradise Lost* Abdiel accuses Satan of now wanting to 'seem patron of liberty, who...Once fawned, and cringed, and servilely adored' his monarch (4: 958). And in Book 6, in his debate with Abdiel just before the battle in heaven, Satan speaks like Milton in the *Readie & Easie Way*: 'At first I thought that liberty and Heav'n | To Heavenly souls had all been one; but now | I see that most through sloth had rather serve...Servility with freedom to contend' (6: 164). In Book 5 Satan undermines the very liberty he espouses with a specious rationale for maintaining hierarchy in the rebellious army 'if not equal all, yet free, | Equally free; for orders and degrees | Jar not with liberty' (*PL* 5: 793). Satan also reveals the bivalency of the term 'right'. 'Who can in reason then or by right assume | Monarchy over such as live by right | His equals' (*PL* 5: 795–96). We begin to agree with Abdiel's deflationary rebuke: 'Shall *thou* dispute | With [God] the points of liberty?' (*PL* 5: 823), only to realize eventually that 'liberty' for

Satan is a disposable notion. Addressing his fellow-rebels half way through the battle in heaven, he praises them as warriors 'Found worthy not of liberty alone, | Too mean pretence, but what we more affect, | Honour, dominion, glory and renown' (*PL* 6: 420). Liberty has become merely a 'mean pretence'. Then, in Book 10, Death compares his bridge to that built by Xerxes across the Hellespont 'the liberty of Greece to yoke', and it is Sin who congratulates her father on extending their domain: 'Thou hast achieved our liberty' (*PL* 10: 368).

Occurrences 10, 11, and 12, however, are different. They are all contained in Michael's lecture on politics in Book 12, within a few lines of each other. Michael explains that liberty in its political sense is, since the Fall, no longer possible. This passage carefully contradicts exactly what Milton had argued, not only in *Tenure*, but in the *First Defense*:

> Therefore since [Man] permits
> Within himself unworthy powers to reign
> Over free reason, God in judgment just
> Subjects him from without to violent lords;
> Who oft as undeservedly enthrall
> His outward freedom: tyranny must be
> Though to the tyrant no excuse.   (*PL* 12: 91–96)

What happens if we apply similar reading techniques to *Paradise Regained* and *Samson Agonistes*? Well, we uncover a lexicon, or its avoidance, that helps to explain the struggles we have had bending these poems to our Whiggish will. Since we all know that *Paradise Regained* is the story, among other things, of how Christ rejected the role of the liberator both of the Israelites and the Romans, I won't dwell on this poem except to remark that the word 'right' *never* appears except in the sense of the implied hereditary right of Christ as understood by Satan: 'Thinkst thou to regain thy right by sitting still' (*PR* 3: 162–63) gibes the Adversary. As for 'liberty', its *only* appearance is in line with Michael's position in *Paradise Lost*, as Christ dismisses the liberationist idea: 'Themselves were they | Who wrought their own captivity...Should I of these the liberty regard?' (*PR* 3: 427). One small note: it is Satan who offers Jesus the temptation of emulating the classical orators (and surely Isocrates must have been on Milton's mind), 'Those ancient, whose resistless eloquence | Wielded at will that fierce **democracy**' (*PR* 4: 268–69). To which the Son replies that the Hebrew prophets are a far better guide to 'the solid rules of civil government' (*PR* 4: 358).

But what about *Samson Agonistes*, the part of the diptych that certain left-wing Miltonists turn to, in hope, if not in despair. Debate on this play has been fiercer, in the era of international terrorism, than on any other work of Milton's. There are some things we can say for sure. The keywords *right* and *rights* do not appear at all in the play, with two exceptions. That is, the Chorus says that those who doubt the justice of God miss the point:

> As if they would confine th'interminable,
> And tie him to his own prescript,
> Who made our laws to bind us, not himself,
> And hath full right to exempt
> Whom so it pleases.   (307–11)

The other instance is even less helpful. It undoes both the divorce pamphlets and their moderation by *Paradise Lost*:

> Therefore God's universal law
> Gave to the man despotic power
> Over his female in due awe,
> Nor from that right to part an hour.   (1053–56)

Not liberty to free himself, but despotic power to keep someone else unfree: and what is more, this is his right with respect to 'his female'. 'His *female*.'

In *Samson Agonistes*, liberty does appear as a word, but no longer as a cause worth fighting for. The Israelites have been brought to 'love bondage more than liberty | Bondage with ease than strenuous liberty' (270–71). When Dalila approaches Samson with the lure of escape from servitude, he replies 'This gaol I count the house of liberty' (948). Manoa, not getting the point, has been busy lobbying the more liberal Philistines, trying 'to work his [son's] liberty' (1454). This is all that *Samson Agonistes* remembers, or tries not to remember, of Milton's favorite political vocabulary.

What does emerge, however, is the newly important presence of the terms 'deliverer' and 'deliverance'. Scattered occasionally through the prose pamphlets, usually in reference to the Long Parliament, appearing in *Paradise Lost* as another way of describing the redemption ('The great deliverance by her seed to come', 12: 600), and in *Paradise Regained* as the misunderstanding of the disciples ('Now, now, for sure, deliverance is at hand', 2: 35), and as the temptation which Christ must reject—the temptation to interpret deliverance in political terms (2: 455; 3: 374), in *Samson*

Agonistes these two words rise to emotional prominence in precisely the sense that is rejected in the companion poem. But
precisely in that sense they are ruled out by what has already
occurred. It is a word of the past. 'Ask for this great deliverer now',
begins Samson with self-flagellating irony, soon to recall that he
married the woman of Timna 'that by occasion hence | I might
begin Israel's deliverance' (325), and to berate those same Israelites
because 'their servile minds | Me their deliverer sent would not
receive' (1214). None of these uses gives 'deliverance' unques-
tioned value. Nor, even as 'God's proposed deliverance' (293),
can it carry the same abstract value as liberty. And if anyone
were to charge Milton, old, blind, and sick, with fomenting
revolutionary ideas against the regime of Charles II by giving his
own version of the Samson story, Milton could and would have
pointed to the two matching assertions by the Chorus, which in
the first edition of the poem faced each other on opposite pages:

> Left: O how comely it is and how reviving
>   To the spirits of just men long oppressed
>   When God into the hands of their deliverer
>   Puts invincible might.   (1268–71)
> Right: *But* patience is more oft the exercise
>   Of saints, the trial of their fortitude,
>   Making them each his own deliverer.   (1287–90)

And the Chorus suggests that though Samson's restored strength
invites the former scenario, his blindness may dictate the latter.

What conclusions are available to us? Did Milton see his poetry
as truly belonging to a different, transcendent realm of thought,

the realm that literary studies *used* to assume was indeed that to which all true literature aspired? Or was he afraid that it would not survive if it fought the battles of the day? Or fought them openly? Was he tempting his readers to read it against the grain? Was he training us to be better readers? Or had Milton reneged on his prose pamphleteering, or on the revolutionary era? This last and more extreme position runs up against his own statement that in *Paradise Lost* he stood defeated but 'unchanged'. True, he still had *Of True Religion* up his sleeve. But his proposed remedy there was only national moral improvement, and study of the bible.

My argument is a compromise. I believe that Milton made a sustained effort, during his entire life, to prevent his poetry from being contaminated by—that is to say, read in the light of—his polemical prose. It is not just that Milton wrote poetry with his right hand and polemic with his left, as he so memorably suggested, but that he either avoided writing poetry that could be smeared by association with his political positions or, if he did write such poetry, as in the case of the four 'commonwealth' sonnets, he chose not to publish it during his lifetime. What he evidently did was to prune and pare the vocabulary of the great poems to make sure that the revolutionary keywords had been bracketed, restricted, or ironized. Consequently, he died in his bed.

Paradise Lost and the D-Word

When Milton pruned his major poems of the great political keywords of his earlier career, he did not abandon the keyword principle. This chapter recognizes not just another, but another *kind* of keyword, not circulating in the public discourse of the day, but brought into prominence by Milton himself and the intensity of his focus, his particular obsessions. For rhetorical suspense, I call this the D-word, and invite you to identify it. If we look to his prose tracts, *Divorce* is obviously a candidate, and the word quickly became associated with Milton's profile as a writer. *Doctrine* was one of Milton's theme words when he started pamphleteering on behalf of the Presbyterians, and it resurfaced both in his first divorce pamphlet and in the *De Doctrina Christiana*, giving it a special status in his internal dictionary. If we think first, as most people do, of *Paradise Lost* we might nominate *Devil*. However, this is a word that Milton almost never uses in his epic, choosing instead, when not simply using the name 'Satan', from a range of more dignified epithets: 'Th'infernal Serpent', 'th'Arch-Enemy', 'Th'Apostate Angel', 'th'Arch-Fiend', 'the superior Fiend', 'the Monarch', 'The Adversary', 'the Prince of Darkness', etc. The conventional word 'devil' as applied to Satan himself appears only five times in *Paradise Lost*, a fact in itself of some interest.

But what then is my D-word? When looking for keywords one can hardly do better than follow the poet's instructions. Remember how *Paradise Lost* begins:

> Of Man's First Disobedience, and the Fruit
> Of that Forbidden Tree, whose mortal tast
> Brought Death into the World, and all our woe,
>
> .   .   .   .
>
> Sing Heav'nly Muse.

Those are Milton's subjects, he tells us plainly, and there in the first line is his first D-word, the First Disobedience. But in fact *disobedience* only occurs five more times in the poem. His second D-word, however, is *Death*, which appears 120 times in *Paradise Lost*. For comparison, Adam appears 88 times, and Eve 95. But these are protagonists. *Death* is only a word. Its frequency alone is remarkable, but it also often appears in circumstances which indicate that Milton is interrogating its usage, clarifying its power, and warding off its danger. Raymond Williams did not include an essay on *Death* in his study of keywords, probably for the reason that by the middle of the twentieth century the word had become taboo. If we don't mention it, perhaps we can avoid it.

The second great word identified in the opening lines of *Paradise Lost* is *World*, which appears 116 times, signaling a different but equally important project: facing the epistemological shifts created for Milton by new cosmologies, the new astronomy, and geographical discoveries of the New World. As

Ayesha Ramanchandran has shown, this was Milton's way of intervening in the daring new speculations associated with Galileo (mentioned in the poem three times), by Descartes in his *Le Monde*, by the new map and globe-makers, and entertained even by Edmund Spenser in the proem to the second book of the *Faerie Queene*. *Paradise Lost* itself describes the making of a new world in Book 7, and toys with Copernican theory in Book 8, using the same speculative phrase, 'What if', that Spenser used to open the imagination to the possibility of 'other worlds' out there in the galaxy. But Milton took the unusual and even retrograde step of bringing the creation story of Genesis back onto center stage, rather than seeing it as just another hypothesis.

For Milton, *World* is an intellectual challenge, but not an alarming one. *Death*, however, is the most fearful, awesome, of all the abstract nouns we possess. Until very late in the poem, Adam and Eve have no idea what *Death*, the punishment they choose to incur, consists of. Neither, it seems, does Satan. But then, one of the theological points of the poem is that fallen angels, poor things, can never die. Presumably God and his Son know what the word means, but Milton is rather shifty on this point. He is absolutely clear, however, on the fact that Adam and Eve have to learn, in stages, what *Death* as an abstract noun can and cannot mean, to them. Milton seems to have intuited that this unintelligibility—our not knowing what 'death' is—is a central fact of the human condition.

This is not such a gloomy topic as one might expect. Among several other projects to which *Paradise Lost* is dedicated, one is thanatology, a grand word that did not enter the English language until the twentieth century. It means the science of death, and now has many ponderous branches. Back then in the seventeenth century, however, they were sometimes smarter than us.

'Men feare *Death*, as Children feare to goe in the darke.' This famous opening sentence marks the arrival of the seventeenth century, as surely as does the good Quarto of *Hamlet*. In 1612, Sir Francis Bacon expanded his *Essays* from the little how-to book he had published at the end of the reign of Elizabeth I, in order to speak more directly to the increasingly modern culture of James I, and his own ambitions therein. The twelve essays previously published were pushed to the bottom of the volume, and the opening essay was now 'Of Death', followed by 'Of Religion'. In 1625 'Of Death' would itself be demoted to second position, trumped by 'Of Truth', which also has a famous opening line: ' "What is Truth", said jesting Pilate, and would not stay for an Answer.' Pilate's gestural dismissal of an absolute criterion for knowledge, or justice, was a proper introduction to the final edition of the *Essays*, for Bacon was not only inaugurating but advertising a shift in attitude. Abstractions—cultural keywords—were now to be subjected to pragmatic and even skeptical scrutiny. But in 1612 this program was already fully evident in 'Of Death', both in its primal position and in the way Bacon handled the topic.

We are often told that the English in the seventeenth century were obsessed with Death. One thinks of John Donne's famous last sermon, or the portrait he had painted of himself in his shroud to stand at the end of his bed, a grisly *memento mori*. But Bacon's essay 'Of Death' is opposed to mental mortification. It is almost cheerful, certainly pedagogic: 'Men feare *Death*, as

Children feare to goe in the darke: and as that Natural Feare in Children, is increased with Tales, so is the other.' That is to say, if we try to train our children to go to bed without the light on, we should train ourselves to live without superstition. Certainly, says Bacon, 'the Contemplation of Death, as the wages of sinne, and Passage to another world, is Holy, and Religious; but the Feare of it, as a Tribute due unto Nature, is weake'. This tension between a religious attitude towards Death and a natural one is the frame of the essay. Towards the end, Bacon writes: 'It is as Naturall to die, as to be borne: And to a little Infant, perhaps, the one is as painfull as the other.' Between these carefully matched statements Bacon suggests that the fear of death has been exaggerated by some forms of Christianity, whereas for him 'that spake onely as a Philosopher, and Naturall Man', that is, Seneca, the culture of Death, groans, friends weeping, etc. terrifies us more than Death itself. Instead, we should think that 'the sweetest Canticle is *Nunc dimittis*; when a Man hath obtained worthy Ends, and Expectations'.

This canny negotiation between faith and reason, religion and the natural, is unexpected so early, even from Bacon the scientist. It takes the sting out of the abstract noun, *Death*, by rendering it less abstract, more simply a physical event. I shall soon argue that Milton aimed at something similar in *Paradise Lost*, though by very different means: by starting with the abstraction in its direst form, and then, by repeating the word *Death* as the name of a puzzle set by God that humans must learn to solve, returning it at last to the status of a natural event, something unfearful, something even to look forward to.

What Bacon and Milton tried to accomplish, modern thanatology has largely undone. In 1972 Robert Kastenberg and Ruth Aisenberg, two psychologists, offered the following conundrum:

> D-E-A-T-H. This sequence of five letters is fixed and familiar. It is easy to assume that the *meaning* of this term is also fixed (unvarying) and familiar (truly known to us). Furthermore, one is tempted to assume that d-e-a-t-h refers to a 'real something' (or a 'real nothing') *out there*. But we never 'really' know what is *out there*. We never even know that there is an *out there* out there. We live within and by our own psychological processes.

These psychologists then proceeded to demonstrate that, within the terms of their discipline, all we can possibly have knowledge about are human *concepts* of death, which, as psychologists, is OK with them. Among such concepts, Bacon might have said, are punishment for sin or travel to a better place. Among the *forms* such concepts may take is allegory. The fact is, and I speak now in my own voice, nobody has any idea what *Death* is, as distinct from dying, which we can continue to observe in others and even in ourselves. Not knowing what *Death* is is crucial, and makes all the difference to *Life*. If complete ignorance were replaced by even partial knowledge, the wager aspect of life would be largely removed, and other huge benefits to society, philosophical thought and introspection, would be trivialized. Compassion would be less necessary. And desire would fail.

Other kinds of scientists have been busy trying to clarify what our concepts of death are, only to further mystify matters. We used to think we knew when death had occurred in others.

Whereas for both Bacon and Milton the moment of death was when breathing and heartbeat stopped, now even this certainty has been undermined. As Walter Jeffko, a philosopher, wrote in 1979, developments in medicine began to pull in two directions:

> First, artificial life-support systems have maintained respiration and circulation in irreversibly comatose individuals whose brain function is totally destroyed... The second development concerns organ transplants. To preserve the vitality of the organ to be transplanted, there should be no unnecessary delay in declaring a person dead. Faced with these two problems the famous Ad Hoc Committee of the Harvard Medical School issued an influential and controversial report in 1968, advocating a 'new' definition of death, that of 'brain death'.

One thing led to another, and shortly there were three competing definitions of *Death* in play, 'the cardiopulmonary', the 'decerebrate', and the 'neocortical'. And in 1980 the American Uniform Determination of Death Act of 1980 actually permitted states to create death statutes with alternative physiological definitions.

In *Paradise Lost* the first speaker to use the D-word other than the Narrator is the allegorical creature Sin, who shouts it out at the moment of the birth of her son, thereby making it his name. But it is not a concept available to the fallen angels. The D-word is not used by Moloch or Belial when debating how they should respond to their military defeat. Moloch says that not much worse can happen if they decide on further fighting: 'more destroy'd than thus | We should be quite abolisht and expire' (2: 92–93), and Belial, from the opposite position, argues the folly of suicidal violence. New conflict 'must end us, that must be our cure, | To be no more' (2: 145–46). To an angel, the only conceivable end is extinction, which is itself inconceivable.

For that reason, if you look for the word *death* in the first two books of the poem, where we see through the eyes of the fallen angels, what stands out is its infrequency. But there is one famous moment—famous at least in literary criticism—when the D-word asserts itself. When Satan goes off on his destructive mission to undermine the newly created human race, the more adventurous of the fallen angels also do some prospecting. What they find are:

Rocks, Caves, Lakes, Fens, Bogs, Dens, and shades of death,
A Universe of death, which God by curse
Created evil, for evil only good,
Where all life dies, death lives, and Nature breeds
Perverse... (2: 621–25)

Here our word appears three times in five lines, and paradox thrills through it: 'all life dies, death lives'. This caught the attention of Edmund Burke, in his famous definition of the Sublime. 'The idea of affection caused by a *word*', wrote Burke, referring to the first mention of *death*,

> which nothing *but* a word could annex to the others, raises a very great degree of the sublime; and it is raised yet higher by what follows, a *'universe of death'*. Here are again two ideas not presentible but by language, and an union of them great and amazing beyond conception.

> Whoever attentively considers this passage in Milton...
> will find that it does not in general produce its end by
> raising the images of things, but by exciting a passion
> similar to that which real objects excite by other instru-
> ments.

'The idea of affection caused by a word'; 'which nothing but a word could annex'; 'two ideas not presentible but by language'. This passage in Burke was cited by Victoria Kahn as part of her brilliant elucidation of the allegory of Sin and Death, a Miltonic visual tour de force with which we must shortly deal. But it seems to me that Burke is talking precisely *not* about 'raising the images of things' as is done by allegory, but rather about how the D-word excites our awe because it is a name for the unre-presentable, our incapacity to know, in the words of the psychologists, whether there is an *out there* out there.

Readers of the poem, however, must, like Satan himself, now come face to face with that allegory, which as everybody knows was Milton's baroque gloss on a few words in the epistle of James: 'Thus when lust hath conceived, it bringeth forth sin: and sin, when it is finished, bringeth forth death.' By underscoring the sexual implications of this biblical text, as distinct from the more familiar 'death is the wages of sin', Milton provided Miltonists with an incentive for a great deal of excitable commentary; but the main issue here is the paradox of representation, the failure even of allegory to do the job. Sin as a woman with distressing lower parts is a sad cliché. But Death is literally indescribable:

The other shape
If shape it might be call'd that shape had none

> Distinguishable in member, joynt, or limb,
> Or substance might be call'd that shadow seem'd,
> For each seem'd either;   (2: 666–70)

The threefold repetition of 'shape' sets that modestly visualizing word in conflict with itself, and Milton also repeats the word 'seem'd' to underline the failure of visualization. When Death threatens his father he 'in shape' (that word again) 'grew tenfold | More dreadful and deform' (705–06). So now we have, in addition to a D-word, a d-form, a science fiction creature. But Milton calls him 'the Goblin', certainly knowing that the word 'goblin' was associated with nursery tales and country superstition. In *Eikonoklastes* he spoke of 'setting aside the affrightment of this Goblin word, Demagogue' (*CPW* 3: 393). Milton also calls Death 'the grisly terror', thus signaling his intentional echo of Spenser's personification of Death in the Mutability Cantos: 'Death with most grim and griesly visage seen'. It will take the rest of Milton's poem to recall the rest of Spenser's definition:

> Yet is he nought but parting of the breath;
> Ne ought to see, but like a shade to ween
> Unbodied, unsoul'd, unheard, unseen.   (7:7:46)

Now, if this were the last we heard and saw of Sin and Death as allegorical figures in the poem my argument would be easier to make. In fact, these nightmare figures will reappear in glee after the Fall, in the first part of Book 10, to claim the world as their domain. The supernatural is not to be replaced so straightforwardly, so chronologically, by the natural. Instead, I think that Milton deliberately created a double-D-word plot: one that works for the religious and superstitious imagination, and one that speaks to the humanists and pragmatists among us. The first of these plots always features Sin-and-Death as a unit; the second decouples them, and concentrates on understanding *Death* as something, in Bacon's words, we owe to nature. But the two plots remain side by side, competing for our attention.

So now let us leave the supernatural and allegorical, and move to the natural part of the poem, our introduction to Adam and Eve. The first human use of the D-word occurs in Book 4, in Adam's first speech to his wife. (It has, by the way, every sign of actually being the very first speech he addresses to her. Yet they were introduced several days ago. 'That day', says Eve, I oft remember.' Perhaps they haven't been doing much talking as yet.) We hear first from Adam about the single prohibition, 'not to taste that onely Tree | Of Knowledge, planted by the Tree of Life, | So neer grows Death to Life, what ere Death is, | Some dreadful thing no doubt' 4: 425–26). *No doubt*. This is really an amazing statement, throwing into disarray precisely what Kastenbaum and Aisenberg noted as the human assumption, that the meaning of D-E-A-T-H is fixed (unvarying) and familiar (truly known to us). And if we, after thousands of years of observing death in others, make this epistemological error, just think how difficult it was for Adam and Eve, who had no such experience.

Satan has overheard. When he returns in Book 9 to begin the temptation of Eve, and Eve, seeing which Tree he has led her to, demurs, Satan deliberately echoes Adam:

> Will God incense his ire
> For such a petty Trespass, and not praise

> Rather your dauntless vertue, whom the pain
> Of Death denounc't, whatever thing Death be,
> Deterrd not from achieving what might leade
> To happier life...

Then he becomes lexically inventive:

> Your feare of Death itself removes the feare.
>
> .   .   .   .   .   .
>
> So shall ye die perhaps, by putting off
> Human, to put on Gods, death to be wisht.
>
> (9: 692–97, 702, 713–14)

This is a neat trick: to redefine a word whose meaning is obscure by suggesting it is merely a metaphor: Death, Satan claims, may just be code for apotheosis. That Eve believes the serpent has himself eaten of the fruit and thereby acquired the human gift of speech lends plausibility to the claim that if she eats it she will be proportionately promoted to a higher stage of being. 'For us alone', she complains, 'was death invented?' speaking more truly than she thought. The results are foreknown. 'Greedily she ingorg'd without restraint, | And knew not eating Death'. This is a very strange and clever locution; it requires a degree of abstract thought that is certainly beyond Eve, and perhaps some readers also.

In the rest of Book 9 both Eve and later Adam engage in a flurry of references to *Death*, and it becomes clear that they have no idea what they are talking about. 'But what if God hath seen,' Eve worries, 'And Death ensue? Then I shall be no more, | And Adam wedded to another Eve, | Shall live with her enjoying, I extinct' (9: 826–29). At this point she imagines non-being as do Moloch and

Belial, as absolute extinction. But a moment later, she says that imagining Adam with another Eve is 'a death to think', reducing the concept to the trivial level of the pangs of jealousy. Next, deciding that whatever happens she will take him with her, she asserts, 'So dear I love him, that with him all deaths | I could endure.' *All deaths*. Pluralization is another form of trivialization. What is plural is no longer a fully abstract noun. When Adam hears her story, he laments her fall in a series of D-words: 'Defac't, deflow'rd, and now to Death devote', thinking evidently in terms of the Proserpina legend and imagining *Death* as *Dis*. In what is for some readers his best moment, he commits himself to share her 'doom': 'If Death | Consort with thee, Death is to me as Life.' But paradox is no solution. And Eve's next speech, congratulating him on his fidelity to her, uses the D-word no less than 5 times in thirty lines, emptying it still further of content with each reiteration. In all, of the 120 appearances of the D-word in the poem, 23 occur in Book 9, the Book of the Fall. But, we might say, it's just the word. All talk and no action. Nobody dies.

And that, indeed, is the problem to which Adam and Eve devote their intelligences in Book 10, which deals with the immediate consequences of the Fall. The first of these consequences is the release of the comic book characters, Sin-and-Death, to start tearing things apart. But in the human sphere, nothing apocalyptic happens. Instead, the D-word becomes the subject of debate. Alone and guilty, Adam bewails the other divine command, 'Increase and multiply' as 'death to hear' (10: 730–31) a metaphor which, like Eve's jealousy, equates *death* with a bad feeling. Then he considers the apparent contradiction between the original decree, which implied that the punishment for disobedience would be immediate, and the manifest fact that he and Eve are still alive. 'Why am I mockt with death, and length'n'd out | To deathless pain?' (10: 774–75). Then he begins to worry that when his body, 'this corporeal Clod', does eventually die, the spirit within it will be unable to die also, and he will 'die a living Death', with the soul buried alive. This problem is technically resolved by invoking the heresy of mortalism—his soul, which was, after all, the part that sinned, will die with his body. But then another thought occurs to Adam:

> But say
> That Death be not one stroke, as I suppos'd,
> Bereaving sense, but endless miserie
> From this day onward . . . ?   (10: 808–11)

This last insight he is able to propound to Eve, after their reconciliation:

> Since this days Death denounc't, if ought I see,
> Will prove no sudden, but a slow-pac'd evill,
> A long days dying to augment our paine   (10: 962–64)

What we need to develop, he says, are coping strategies: 'how we may light'n | Each other's burden in our share of woe'. In this, the saddest of all human conversations, the D-word appears 16 times. But it also marks the beginning of Milton's version of Bacon's essay *Of Death*.

Indeed, Book 11 takes, as it were, a deep breath and changes everything. First, God the Father explains that, actually, Death is now not a threat but a gift to fallen man:

> I at first with two fair gifts
> Created him endow'd, with Happiness
> And Immortalie; that fondly lost,
> This other serv'd but to eternize woe;
> Till I provided Death; so Death becomes
> His final remedie...   (11: 57–62)

Shrewdly, however, the Father sends the archangel Michael to drive the fallen pair from Eden lest they poach also from the Tree of Life and so regain, by outsmarting God, the immortality they have lost.

Up to this point, all that Adam and Eve have as the content for the D-word is delay. Whatever thing *Death* may be, it didn't happen when they thought it would. Now Adam at least will get to experience it vicariously, which is as far as our human experience of it goes, but in this, the very first case, it must also be proleptically. In prospect, Michael shows Adam the first fratricide, the slaughter by Cain of Abel, gushing blood and all. Adam cries out, naively: 'But have I now seen Death? Is this the way | I must return to native dust?' Are all human deaths to be violent like this one?

> To whom thus Michael. Death thou hast seen
> In his first shape on man; but many shapes
> Of Death, and many are the wayes that lead
> To his grim Cave...   (11: 466–70)

If we remember Milton's play on the word 'shape' in his description of Death as an allegorical figure, we can see this passage as answering and improving on the previous one.

Precisely because there are many shapes of Death, none can be quite so scary as their formless or deformed abstraction. And watch how carefully Michael finishes his point. 'Many are the ways that lead | To his grim Cave, all dismal; yet to sense | More terrible at th'entrance then within.' In this extraordinary statement, the archangel offers comfort similar to Bacon's. It may be painful when we begin to die, by whatever means, and we are terrified; but once the threshold is passed, pain itself dies away.

Michael then proceeds to list some of the ways in which men and women in the real world experience death:

> Some, as thou saw'st, by violent stroke shall die,
> By Fire, Flood, Famine, by Intemperance more
> In Meats and Drinks, which on the Earth shall bring
> Diseases dire... (11: 471–74)

And then, to fill out the D-word *Disease* with some physical content, Adam is shown a hospital, and surveys the maladies from which the inhabitants suffer. It is well known that Milton's catalog of diseases derives from Du Bartas's *Divine Weeks*, a poem so devoted to the encyclopedic form of knowledge that his Adam is himself implausibly attacked by every disease known to man (including anorexia and bulimia) for a depressing two hundred and some lines. Milton chose a few of the same examples, homely ones to our ears—epilepsy, catarrh, stone, colic, dropsy, asthma, and rheumatism—but contained the episode within a mere twenty lines, leaving out the most outlandish conditions. Yet he had room in those twenty lines for something not mentioned by Du Bartas: 'despair | Tended the sick busiest from Couch to Couch.'

> And over them triumphant Death his Dart
> Shook, but delaid to strike, though oft invok't,
> With vows, as thir chief good and final hope.   (11: 490–93)

This may strike you as a bleak idea of a chief good. But when Adam asks, quite reasonably: 'Is there yet no other way, besides | These painful passages, how we may come | To Death, and mix with our connatural dust?', Michael completes the lesson on a much more upbeat note:

> There is, said Michael, if thou well observe
> The rule of not too much, by temperance taught,
>
> .   .   .   .
>
> Till many years over thy head return:

Or, to quote Woody Allen, 'You can live to be a hundred if you give up all the things that make you want to live to be a hundred.'

> So maist thou live, till like ripe Fruit thou drop
> Into thy Mothers lap, or be with ease
> Gatherd, not harshly pluckt, for death mature.   (11: 530–37)

Thus the 'Fruit of the Forbidden Tree' turns into the 'ripe Fruit' of a healthy human old age; and Milton comes full circle, also, from the opening lines of *Lycidas*: 'I come to pluck your Berries harsh and crude, | And with forc'd fingers rude, | Shatter your leaves before the mellowing year.'

Admittedly this lovely image is somewhat undercut by Michael's follow-up: 'This is old age', of which he gives a dim picture. Nevertheless, Adam responds:

> Henceforth I flie not Death, nor would prolong
> Life much, bent rather how I may be quit
> Fairest and easiest of this combrous charge,
> Which I must keep till my appointed day
> Of rendring up, and patiently attend
> My dissolution.   (11: 547–52)

I like the word 'patiently' here. It points back to the 'better fortitude | of Patience and Heroic Martyrdom' (9: 31–32) by which Milton in old age replaced the military values of traditional epic. It echoes the ethos of Sonnet 19, where Milton in mid-life crisis received a lesson from an allegorical Patience: 'They also serve who only stand and wait', she said or he said, rather unpersuasively. But to hear Adam anticipating involuntary longevity as his biggest test in the world outside the Garden is to receive more helpful, truly mature advice. Ethically, it almost improves, if anything could, on 'the sweetest canticle', the 'Nunc dimittis', invoked by Sir Francis Bacon, words spoken by an old man who has finished his life's work and has finally been granted a vision of what it meant.

There is no other poem by Milton that takes such interest in the *idea*, however shapeless, inscribed in the abstract noun *Death*—bar one. The abstraction never appears in *Lycidas*, though the concrete state of being 'dead' tolls twice in the opening lines, and once towards the end, only to be denied. *Mors* never appears in the more than 200 lines of Latin epitaph for Charles Diodati, which as formal avoidance is really an achievement. But the exception is a big surprise—the comic epitaph that

Milton wrote for Thomas Hobson, the university carrier, in 1632. Somewhat absurdly, this will be the one poem quoted here in entirety:

> Here lies old Hobson, Death hath broke his girt,
> And here, alas, hath laid him in the dirt.
> Or else the ways being foul, twenty to one,
> He's stuck here in a slough, and overthrown.
>
> 'Twas such a shifter, that if truth were known,
> Death was half glad when he had got him down;
> For he had any time this ten years full,
> Dodg'd with him, betwixt Cambridge and the Bull.
> And surely, Death could never have prevail'd,
> Had not his weekly course of carriage fail'd;
> But lately finding him so long at home,
> And thinking now his journey's end was come,
> And that he had ta'en up his latest Inn,
> In the kind office of a Chamberlain
> Show'd him his room where he must lodge that night,
> Pull'd off his Boots, and took away the light:
> If any ask for him, it shall be said,
> Hobson has supt, and's newly gone to bed.

This charming poem, which Milton published in his first collected volume in 1645/6, succeeds even better than Bacon's essay in taking away the fear of Death, mentioned though he be, with a capital D, three times in the poem's mere sixteen lines (two more than a sonnet, exactly matching the epitaph for Shakespeare). There is personification allegory here, obviously, but

now the grim specter performs 'the kind office of a Chamber-
lain', even pulling off the old man's boots for him and tucking
him into bed. Hobson's long life of service—he died on New
Year's Day, 1631, at the age of 86, and having taken over his
father's carrier business in 1564—puts him, though Milton does
not make this point, in the category of those old men, like the
Simeon of 'Nunc dimittis', who have earned their rest. The
conceit that Death, who has been chasing Hobson for years,
only catches him because he has had to stay home for a few days
(London was in the grip of the plague) is, as a metaphor of the
hunt, quickly disarmed. Hobson is not prey, but welcome guest.
It is Hobson, not Death, who has 'sup't', and what shall be said
of him is simply that he is 'gone to bed', words of native (Anglo-
Saxon) plainness and comfort.

It Is Written. *Paradise Regained*: Words that Count

Keywords count as flashpoints in debate, as convenient short-hand for large ideas. But for a writer like Milton who lived in a world still largely governed by religious belief, there was another kind of word that clearly outranked keywords, however powerful. These were the words known, however misleadingly, as Scripture. In one of his last poems, Milton confronted the special status of biblical texts, and discovered, or uncovered, a huge dilemma. *Paradise Regained* is that poem, which gives it, too, special status in his canon.

In the second book of the *Reason of Church Government*, published early in 1642, Milton had publicly addressed his literary ambitions and qualifications. Having in *Animadversions* engaged in hand-to-hand conflict with an English bishop, though anonymously, Milton now decided to appear in his own person in the newly exciting public sphere. He was coming out. This new tract carried his name on the title page: Mr John Milton; and this hitherto unknown writer proceeded to advertise himself in extraordinarily grand terms. First, he told his readers why he felt himself in line to be the next great national poet; and second, why he was currently tied up in controversy, which of course required him to write in prose. This is where he formulated the famous definition of his second best activity, a rating that has encouraged his readers for hundreds of years to ignore his prose works:

> Lastly, I should not chuse this manner of writing wherin knowing myself inferior to my self, led by the genial power of nature to another task, I have the use, as I may account it, but of my left hand.   (*CPW* 1: 808)

But duty calls; in the meantime, Milton makes a preemptive strike for a permanent place in the literary pantheon. His Italian friends have encouraged him to think that he 'might perhaps leave *something so written* to aftertimes, as they should not willingly let it die' (*CPW* 1: 810; italics added). He has therefore determined 'to fix all the industry and art I could unite to the adorning of my native tongue' (811). His models will be the great writers of Athens, Rome, or modern Italy, and he hopes also that what 'those Hebrews of old did for their country, I in my proportion with this over and above of being a Christian, might doe for mine' (812). No other piece of writing by Milton is so concerned with the act of writing, or with his duty to the vernacular.

One would think, therefore, that by the time he had fulfilled that intermediate duty—the work of the left hand—in grander terms than he could have imagined in 1642; by the time he had (almost) abandoned prose polemic; by the time he had burst upon the world as the author of the greatest poem that Englishmen had seen for generations—Milton would have figured out what his own literary theory was. We can see from *Paradise Regained*, however, that this was far from the case.

As Jesus replied to Satan in the third temptation:

> ... if I would delight my private hours
> With Music or with Poem, where so soon
> As in our native Language can I find
> That solace?   (4: 331–34)

In this context 'our native Language' is, of course, Hebrew, and the poetry Jesus has in mind is found primarily in the Psalms. Jesus also explicitly rejected 'all the Oratory of Greece and Rome' (4: 360) as a guide to statesmanship, preferring 'our Prophets | As men divinely taught, and better teaching | The solid rules of Civil Government' (4: 356–58). How was this ideal compatible with those outlined in the *Reason of Church Government*? Clearly, it was not. Did Milton realize this? Of course. Did he, in *Paradise Regained*, solve the problem of their incompatibility? No, he rather highlighted it.

At the heart of the problem he could not solve was the question implied by my title: which are the words that really count? Any reader of *Paradise Regained* has noticed its greater reliance on and fidelity to Scripture—that is to say, to the actual words of the bible—than we find in *Paradise Lost*, most of which Milton simply invented. In theory, Milton espoused a rigorous scripturalism as the test of and mainstay of belief. A rigorous scripturalism is not the same as a literal scripturalism, obviously, and Milton's divorce pamphlets are exercises in how to make Scripture mean what you want it to mean. But a rigorous scripturalism in poetry is, if not oxymoronic, self-incriminating. The bible makes poetry, even poetry based on the bible, trivial, unnecessary.

What is Scripture? Obviously, something written down—in special circumstances, and by special people. I want to argue here that *Paradise Regained* was originally conceived within a specifically Protestant program, an essay on the importance of reading the Scriptures, which acquired their authority by having been written. Its hero, Jesus, was himself an ardent scriptural exegete. His survival of the Temptation in the Wilderness was thanks to this self-education in what *he* knew as Scripture, that is, the Old Testament. Each of Satan's three offers, to accept any one of which would render him impotent as a redeemer, is rebutted by Jesus by way of a citation from the Old Testament, each of which is prefaced with the phrase, 'it is written'. What could be simpler? In the long course of the poem's life, however, this fundamentalist approach would become compromised by another imperative, the need to produce a sequel to *Paradise Lost*. The poem's compositional history, as we know and guess it, suggests late revision in a direction incompatible with the original concept. But from the start there was a problem of textual authority, to which I turn first.

Scripture's Unreliability

For the basic plot of *Paradise Regained*, the New Testament story of the temptation of Jesus in the wilderness, there is no single source-text, but rather three different accounts: the extremely brief (two verses) mention in Mark, which the consensus of modern scholarship now believes to be the earliest; and the two much longer, obviously closely related accounts in Matthew and Luke, whose similarities are to be accounted for either by the hypothesis that Luke had access to Matthew's gospel, or that they shared a common source (the theory of a Q text), or some combination of the two. What both Matthew and Luke introduce is a story of three temptations, remarkable for being incredible, since, of all the episodes in the life of Jesus described in the gospels, this is the only one for which there were no witnesses! There could be no witnesses, because the terrible isolation of Jesus in the wilderness was a central part of the test. The importance of eyewitnesses as testimony to the truth of the New Testament is remarked by Luke in the preface to his gospel. Therefore, unless we are to posit the unlikely hypothesis that Jesus later told this story to one of the apostles, which would have been extraordinarily self-regarding, this episode fails Luke's own test of authenticity.

In its focus on Jesus' citation of the Old Testament, however, this is a brilliant paradigm of the tactics early Christianity learned to use in its scheme for self-validation. The early Christian Jews reviewed the Jewish Scriptures, adopted them as their pre-history, and made them not only into the Old Testament (a prequel) but a *textual* corroboration of the New. This goal is explicit in Luke 24: 25–27, which makes Jesus himself the author of this takeover. After his resurrection, on the road to Emmaus, he rebukes the two disciples whom he met on the road with their skepticism:

> Then he said unto them O fooles and slowe of heart to believe [literally] all that the Prophetes have spoken ... And he began at Moses, & all the Prophetes, and interpreted

> unto them in all the Scriptures the things which were
> written of him.

'In all the Scriptures the things which were written of him'. This is the criterion which Jesus himself adopted as a guide to his own behavior and future.

The story of the Temptation material is unlikely to have derived from the hypothetical Q text, which most biblical scholars who believe in it agree to have been a collection of Jesus' 'sayings' (*kerygma*) accumulated in oral tradition, and written down not only long after the historical life of Jesus, but also after the Jewish captivity and the actual destruction of the Temple. All of Mark, Matthew, and Luke share the literary impulse to make a collection of 'sayings' into a *Life*. Mark, however, focuses on the death of Jesus, to which everything else looks forward. Matthew's great contribution was the account of the Nativity, the flight into Egypt, and the Massacre of the Innocents, not only one of the world's greatest narratives (because it featured babies), but one that allowed the evangelist to enlist Isaiah 7: 14, Hosea 11: 1, and Jeremiah 31: 15. So now the *Life* had a beginning as well as an ending. Luke omits the flight into Egypt and the Masssacre, and adds the Annunciation, creating another debt to Isaiah 7: 4. He also increased the familial emphasis, by adding the conception of John the Baptist by a similar miraculous intervention. In fact, given the space Luke devotes to the Baptist's birth as compared to that of Jesus, he (John) might well have been assumed in the opening chapters to have been the hero of the ensuing narrative. What distinguishes the Temptation episode, however, is its nearly identical telling by Matthew and Luke; by its emphasis not on 'sayings' but on a narrative framework—a narrative, moreover, that exhibits the triple-test structure of folklore, which in folktales usually follows a miraculous birth. Mark had no idea of any of this. It must have been quite a late addition to the evolving Christology, which became more miraculous as it grew.

Though close, Matthew and Luke had some disagreement. Whereas Matthew has the temptations in this order: stones into bread, pinnacle of the temple, kingdoms of the world, Luke has instead: stones into bread, kingdoms of the world, and pinnacle of the temple. In addition, Matthew states that after the third temptation, 'the devil left him, and beholde, the Angels came and ministred unto him' (4: 11). Luke's climax is merely as follows: 'And when the devil had ended all the tentacion, he departed from him for a season' (4: 13). Matthew implies a victory with rewards, Luke merely a cessation. But what Milton did about these divergences is crucial, and we must attend to it in some detail.

Milton himself knew that the most basic principle of the Reformation, *sola scriptura*, was implicitly challenged by the already well-developed science of biblical textual criticism. In *De Doctrina Christiana* he declares that, due to *its* processes of composition, the New Testament is less reliable than the Old. It 'is, in fact, corrupt':

> This has come about because it has been committed to the care of various untrustworthy authorities, has been collected together from an assortment of divergent manuscripts, and has survived in a medley of transcripts and editions... We possess no autograph copy: no exemplar

which we can rely on as more trustworthy than others. Thus Erasmus, Beza and other learned men have edited from the various manuscripts what seems to them to be the most authentic text. I do not know why God's providence should have committed the contents of the New Testament to such wayward and uncertain guardians, unless it was so that this very fact might convince us that the Spirit which is given to us is a more certain guide than scripture, and that we ought to follow it.

(*CPW* 6: 588–89)

This is not a very neat escape from an insuperable Reformation Catch-22. Later, the challenge would be more directly faced by Father Richard Simon, a Catholic, whose *Critical History of the New Testament* appeared in English in 1689 and, against its own intentions, provided many of the arguments for deism. Simon, for example, dealt carefully with the most likely chronology of the phase in the early Christian church when oral tradition became written, and took a rather pragmatic view of that process:

'Tis not necessary, for a Book's being inspired, that it should be indited by God, word for word.... Jesus Christ, who promised to his Apostles that the Spirit of God should guide them in all the functions of their Ministry, did not therefore deprive them of their Reason and Memory: Although they were inspired, they continued to be Men still, and managed their Affairs as other Men. I freely own, that there was no need of inspiration, to put in record such matters of Fact, whereof they themselves were Witnesses. But this does not hinder, but

> they were directed by the Spirit of God in all that they put
> in Writing, so as not to fall into error.   (p. 61)

Thus Father Simon smoothly erased the difference between first-hand reports and other parts of the gospels, while avoiding the presumption that divine inspiration informed the evangelists of what they could not have witnessed.

But he did not apply this commonsense approach to the particular problem of the Temptation, for which there *could* have been no witnesses if the story were to ring true in another, characterological sense. Unlike the last verses of Mark, or the story of the woman taken in adultery, which Milton himself refers to as a corruption (*CPW* 6: 589), the authenticity of both the Matthew and Luke versions of the Temptation seems to have been a problem hiding in plain sight. Thomas Paine, eighteenth-century skeptic, eventually picked up on this anomaly. Paine, who believed that Jesus was a historical person, knew that this story was egregious fiction, but focused only on its most improbable moment:

> The most extraordinary of all the things called miracles, related in the New Testament, is that of the devil flying away with Jesus Christ, and carrying him to the top of a high mountain, and to the top of the highest pinnacle of the temple, and showing him and promising to him all the kingdoms of the world. How happened it that he did not discover America, or is it only with kingdoms that his sooty highness has any interest? I have too much regard for the moral character of Christ to believe that he told this whale of a miracle himself; neither is it easy to account for

what purpose it could have been fabricated, unless it were…to render the belief of miracles ridiculous, by outdoing miracles, as Don Quixote outdid chivalry.

(*Age of Reason*, 1: 14)

Deuteronomy

We now need to examine the most peculiar feature of the Matthew and Luke accounts of the Temptation: the threefold citation of the Old Testament as the magic 'sayings' on which Jesus can rely to deliver him from temptation. My text for these citations, as for the earlier one, is the Geneva bible, published in 1560, because it appealed in its glosses to a Protestant readership. What were the magic texts? Both Matthew and Luke set this up as a test for the reader, who would have to be his own scriptural scholar; but for post-Reformation readers the Geneva bible supplies assistance. I will cite Luke, for that was the choice that Milton made in adopting the story as his own:

> And Jesus full of the holie Gost returned from Jordan, and was led by the Spirit into the wilderness,
>
> And was there fourtie dayes tempted of the devil, and in those days he did eat nothing: but when they were ended, he afterwarde was hungrie.
>
> Then the devil said unto him, If thou be the Sonne of God, commande this stone that it be made bread.
>
> But Jesus answered him, saying, *It is written*, That man shal not live by bread onely, but by everie worde of God. (my italics)

The Geneva bible here glosses *It is written*, with a reference to Deuteronomy 8: 3, to which if we turn we find something marvelously apropos: 'Therefore he humbleth thee, and made thee hungry, & fed thee with Man[na] which thou knewst not, neither did thy fathers knowe it, that he might teache thee that man liveth not by bread onely, but by everie *worde* that proceadeth out of the mouth of the Lord, doeth a man live.' (Italics original, signifying the translator's interpolation.) Thus the first temptation constitutes a subtle exercise in exegesis, an exercise played by Jesus upon the original strings which include the word 'word'. Deuteronomy supplies the play on Manna and man, the antithesis of bread and *worde*, Jesus supplies the verbal sign of biblical quotation, *It is written*, which permits him to answer his Tempter merely in the words of Moses, now made his own.

Now the second temptation:

> Then the devil toke him up into an high mountaine, and shewed him all the Kingdoms of the worlde, in the twinkeling of an eye.
>
> And the devil said unto him, All this power wil I give thee, and the glorie of those kingdomes . . . If thou therefore will worship me, they shal be all thine.
>
> But Jesus answered him, and said, 'Hence from me, Satan: *for it is written*, Thou shalt worship the Lord thy God, and him alone shalt thou serve. (italics mine)

And again the Geneva marginal note directs us to Deuteronomy, 6: 16 and 10: 20, which Jesus has welded together into a single quotation, the two original prescripts for monotheism having become one. And then the third temptation:

> Then he brought him to Jerusalem, and set him on a
> pinnacle of the Temple, and said unto him, If thou be the
> Sonne of God, cast thy self downe from hence, For *it is
> written* That he wil give his Angels charge over thee to
> kepe thee: And with their handes they shal lift thee up,
> lest at anie time thou shuldest dash thy foot against a
> stone. (italics mine)

In other words, Satan has learned from Jesus the efficacy of the
biblical quotation in establishing authority. His quotation is
from Psalm 91: 12, and it has a deceptively comforting ring:

> And Jesus answered and said unto him, *It is said,*
> [though Matthew has '*It is written againe*'] Thou shalt
> not tempt the Lord thy God. (italics mine)

That was all; but the Geneva gloss explains that this is, in fact,
Jesus' third quotation from Deuteronomy (6: 16). Again, if we
check, we find: 'Ye shal not tempt the Lord your God, as ye did
tempt him in Massah.' And the margin adds: 'by douting of his
power, refusing lawful meanes, & abusing his graces'.

In patristic commentary, that is to say, Roman Catholic tradition, the three temptations were usually explained as being about
something *we* might recognize as a sin: stones into bread appeals
to gluttony; kingdoms of the world, to avarice; pinnacle of the
temple, to vainglory. But the real issues in the scriptural account
are simply two: Satan's desire to test the meaning of the phrase
'Son of God' (which is emphasized in the first and the third
temptations by the phrase 'If thou be the Sonne of God'), and
the Son's refusal to answer all three temptations except in terms of

quotations from Deuteronomy, a strategy which brings Satan to three dead ends. It is not *what* Jesus refuses but *how* he refuses that matters. And this emphasis fitted much better with an evolving Protestant exegetics.

The phrase, 'It is written', is found so many times in the Old Testament that it there forgoes any epistemological or ontological significance. Here it has been rescued from banality and made central to how the New Testament relates to the Old—as pupil, or perhaps we should say disciple. The wittiest part of the story is, perhaps, the fact that Satan is shown to be a quick learner, adapting the *it is written* formula to his own ends. The Temptation, then, as relayed by both Matthew and Luke, is a contest of wits. Both contestants make the same assumption, that being written constitutes authority. Implicitly, they also debate the question of whether some books of the Old Testament have greater authority than others. Evidently, words attributed to Moses trump those attributed to David. We should note that Mark had already given the phrase 'it is written' new and prophetic significance in his own short gospel. At the cleansing of the Temple, 'he taught, saying unto them, *Is it not written*, Mine House shalbe called the House of prayer unto all nacions? But you have made it a denne of theves' (italics mine). The Geneva bible supplies the references to Isaiah 56: 7 and Jeremiah 7: 11. Thus the concept of the New Testament as leaning on the Old *by way of Jesus' own biblical scholarship* was already established. But the move made by Matthew and Luke, however related to each other, was to take this principle two steps further: to propose that Deuteronomy had special ranking, as the words of God himself as conveyed through Moses, and to make the *it is written* formula an essential ingredient of narrative structure. Though the threefold test was one of the most common features of primitive narrative, seldom does it appear with such a clear deictic.

John Bale

The Geneva bible was preceded in its interpretation of the Temptation by a very early English Reformer, one who became a famous figure in the conversion of Catholic writings to Protestant uses. John Bale was John Milton's most significant predecessor in turning the biblical account of the Temptation in the Wilderness into literature, specifically drama. I will propose here that Milton may have known Bale's play, and that play-form was one of the stages through which *Paradise Regained* passed before becoming Milton's penultimate poem. Bale was a Carmelite monk who converted to Protestantism in about 1534/5, at the very moment when the Henrician Reformation was first stirring. By 1536 Henry had begun to fear that political would become doctrinal reform, which must be held at bay by the Ten Acts, and in January of the following year Bale was charged with heresy before John Stokesly, the conservative bishop of London. He was saved by the intervention of Thomas Cromwell, on account of his plays ('*ob editas comoedias*'), an important record, since it tells us that some of his plays were already written. Bale set out to replace the English Catholic mystery plays with Protestant equivalents, and had early success. Thereafter he fell athwart of the wave of conservative reaction that resulted in the Six Articles of 1539, the dissolution of the marriage between the king and Anne of Cleves, which would have cemented England's Protestant alliances, and the resulting execution of his protector, Thomas Cromwell. Bale fled to Europe, returning in 1548 to take part in the Edwardian Reformation.

Before he left Europe, however, he saw to the reprinting of the *Temptacyon of Christ* by the press of Dirk van der Straten, otherwise known as T. Plateanus, at Wesel in 1547. Even though there is only one surviving copy, in the Bodleian Library, it is possible that another had crossed Milton's path. (One can understand why such a rebellious text would disappear. There are only three surviving copies of Milton's own *Readie & Easie Way* in the second edition.) Bale himself was a stubborn survivor. When Mary replaced Edward, Bale organized a public performance of his three Protestant mystery plays, including the *Temptacyon*, on the very day of the local celebrations for Mary's accession. Again he left hurriedly for Europe, and again he returned when Elizabeth succeeded her sister.

Bale conceived of his *Temptacyon* as a comedy, and indeed it has strongly comic aspects. The 'Interlocutores' consists of Jesus Christus, Satan tentator, Angelus primus, Angelus alter, and Baleus Prolocutor, or Bale himself acting as the Prologue. Here is that prologue:

> After hys baptyme Christ was Gods sonne declared
> By the fathers voice as ye before have hearde,
> Whych sygnyfyeth to us, that we ones baptysed
> Are the sonnes of God, by hys gift & rewarde.
> And because that we, shuld have Christ in regarde,
> He gave unto hym, *the mighty autoryte,*
> *Of hys heavenly worde, our only teacher to be.* (italics mine)

Thus Bale's opening premise is a strong Reformation scripturalism, along with a generous interpretation of what it means to
be a son of God.

Balus Prolocutor continues:

> Now is he gone fourth, into the desert place,
> With the holy Ghost, hys offyce to begynne.

HIS OFFICE TO BEGIN. Surely a very important locution,
especially with 'begynne' in the rhyme word position. That word
is key in *Paradise Regained*. In Book 1, Jesus describes the
baptism as telling him 'the time | Now full, that I no more
should live obscure, | But openly begin' (1: 287–89). In Book 2,
Jesus 'Into himself descended, and at once | All his great work to
come before him set; | How to begin' (2: 111–13). In Book 3, Satan
grasps the significance of the word, but not of the chronology:
'The happier reign the sooner it begins' (3: 179) he will urge, and
Jesus will reply, first and crucially: 'If of my reign Prophetic Writ
hath told | That it shall never end, so when begin | The Father in
his purpose hath decreed', and then, tauntingly, 'But what
concerns it thee when I begin . . . Knowst thou not that my
rising is thy fall'. And at the very end of *Paradise Regained* the
angelic chorus advises Jesus: 'on thy glorious work | Now enter,
and begin to save mankind'. Thus the word which is practically
Bale's beginning is at the heart of the argument in *Paradise
Regained*, and its last appearance, as we shall see, is its most
important.

Both Bale and Milton speak to the interpretive tradition that
the Temptation in the Wilderness *was* the beginning of the

ministry. Bale expected the *Temptacyon* to be performed right after his other interlude, *Johann Baptystes Preachyng*. Unlike the miracle plays, Bale articulates the tradition that it was precisely this proclamation by the Baptist that alerted Satan to his new peril. When Satan Tentator enters, he tells the audience:

I hearde a great noyse in Jordan now of late,
Upon one Jesus, soundynge from heaven above:
'Thys is myne owne sonne which hath withdrawne al hate,
And he that doth stande most hyghly in my love'.
My wyttes the same sounde doth not a lyttle move;
He cometh to redeme the kynde of Man, I feare.
Hygh tyme is it than for me the cooles to steare [i.e. to stir the coals].

Here is the germ of Milton's scene in Book 1 (ll. 33–105) which begins, 'That heard the Adversary', in which Satan carries the news of the Baptism to an infernal conference, and declares that this new and threatening development 'must with something sudden be opposed'. 'Who this is we must learn', says Milton's Satan; and Bale's Satan continues:

> I wyll not leave hym tyll I knowe what he ys,
> And what he entendeth in thys same border heare.
> Subtyltie must helpe, els all wyll be amys:
> A godly pretence outwardly must I beare,
> Semynge relygouse, devoute and sad in my geare.

And then there is a stage direction in Latin: *Hic simulata religione Christum aggreditur*. Likewise Milton's Satan announces that he will have to use 'not force, but well-couched fraud, well woven snares'. Shortly he will appear as 'an aged man in Rural weeds'.

Bale does not specify precisely what outfit *simulata religione* entails, but his Satan does introduce himself as a 'brother of this desert wyldernesse', and later explicitly as a hermit, so that he can pretend *not* to have access to biblical learning, i.e. no library:

> Scriptures I knowe non, for I am but an hermyte, I.
> We relygyouse men lyve all in contemplacyon.
> Scriptures to stodye is not our occupacyon;
> It longeth to doctours.

As we shall see, this is doubly a lie, first in that Satan is no hermit, and secondly in that he *has* studied the Old Testament. Now Bale moves promptly to the first temptation:

> Satan tentator.
> Well, to be playne with you, abroade the rumour doth ronne
> Among the people, that ye shuld be Gods sonne.
> Yf ye be Gods sonne, as it hath great lykelyhode,
> Make of these stones breade, and geve your bodye hys fode.
> Jesus Christus.
> Ye speake in that poynt, very unadvysedlye,
> For it is written, in the eyt of Deutronomye,
> Man lyveth not by breade, or corporall fedynge onlye,
> But by Gods promyse, and by hys scriptures heavenlye.
> Here ye persuade me, to recreate my bodye,
> And neglecte Gods worde, whych is great blasphemye.

Here Bale has performed, on our behalf, the necessary piece of biblical criticism. His Jesus not only answers by way of a quotation from Deuteronomy, but *explains that he is citing*

Deuteronomy. In *Paradise Regained* Milton's Jesus gives the same answer much more economically, by returning to the actual words of Deuteronomy, which, as we have seen, play Word against Bread:

> Is it not written
>
> .   .   .   .
>
> Man lives not by Bread only, but each Word
> Proceeding from the mouth of God, who fed
> Our Fathers here with Manna?

Both Bale and Milton thus give us in the first temptation a Jesus who is a biblical exegete, careful to cite his sources; and Milton develops this idea by having the Son, in the first book of *Paradise Regained*, describe his childhood education in the 'Law of God', and how, after the vision at his Baptism, he returned to the source: 'Straight I again revolv'd | The Law and Prophets, searching what was writ | Concerning the Messiah, to our Scribes | Known partly, and soon found of whom they spake, | I am (1: 259–62). This brilliant use of enjambement to create surprise, to create revelation, goes well beyond Bale.

Having been defeated in the first temptation, Bale's Satan (who is working with the order of the temptations in Matthew, remember), proposes to take Christ to the Holy City of Jerusalem. This is nicely handled as a satirical rebuke to Jesus for his excessive self-denial:

> No meate wyll ye eate, but lyve by Gods word onlye,
> So good are ye wext so parfyght and so holye
>
> .   .   .   .

Here is all holy, here is the holy cytie,
The holy temple, and the holy prestes here be,
Ye wyll be holy? Wel, ye shall be above them all,
Bycause ye are Gods sonne, it doth ye so befall.
Come here, on the pynnacle we wyll be by and by.

When Jesus asks what he is up to, Satan shows that he has learned a new strategy from his adversary:

When ye were hungrye, I did ye first persuade,
Of stones to make breade, but ye wolde non of that trade.
Ye layed for your self, that scripture wolde not serve it.
That was your bucklar, but now I am for ye fyt.
For the suggestyon, that I now shall to ye laye,
I have scripture at hande, ye shall it not denaye.

. . . .

If ye do beleve, that ye are the sonne of God,
Beleve thys also, if ye leape downe here in scoff,
From thys hygh pynnacle, ye can take no harme thereoff.

. . . .

If ye be Gods sonne, cast downe your self here backwarde.

Backwards is a nice touch, unbiblical, but entirely appropriate to the tone that Bale's Satan has now adopted. This is, after all, a comedy.

But Bale has more to extract from this temptation and its rejection than Scripture alone could offer:

Jesus Christus.
Truly that nede not, here is other remedy

To the grounde to go, than to fall downe folyshlye
Here are gresynges [i.e. steps] made, to go up and downe
thereby,
What nede I than leape, to the earthe presumptuously.

.   .   .   .

Satan tentator.
Tush, scripture is with it, ye can not fare amys.
For it is written, how God hath geven a charge,
Unto hys Angels, that if ye leape at large,
They shall receyve ye, in their handes tenderly,
Least ye dashe your fote, agaynst a stone thereby.

What Bale does with Satan's clever move is quite extraordinary. Instead of leaping, as does the Son in Matthew, straight to the warning from Deuteronomy 'Thou shalt not tempt the Lord thy God', a rebuke of such minimalist inscrutability that Milton was able to make it the turning point of his poem, Bale at this point has his Satan and his Christ engage in a debate on the principles of biblical exegesis, which needs to be quoted in its entirety:

Jesus Christus.
In no wyse ye oughte, the scriptures to deprave.
But as they ly whole, so ought ye them to have.
Nor more take ye here, than serve for your vayne purpose
Leavynge out the best, as ye shuld tryfle or glose,
Ye mynde not by this, towardes God to edyfye,
But of syncere fayth to corrupt the innocency.
Satan tentator.
Whye, is it not true, that soch a text there is?

Jesus Christus.
Yea, there is soch a text, but ye wrast it all amys.
As the Psalme doth saye, God hath commaunded Angels,
To preserve the just, from daungerous plages and [perils].
Satan tentator.
Well than, I sayd true, and as it lyeth in the text.
Jesus Christus.
Yea, but **ye omitted foure wordes** whych foloweth next,
As (in all thy wayes) whych if ye put out of syght,
Ye shall never take, that place of scripture aryght.

The Geneva bible shows that this was the standard Protestant
interpretation: 'He [Satan] alledgeth but halfe the sentence to
deceive thereby the rather, and cloke his craftie purpose.' And
then Bale's Jesus rebuts Bale's funniest line:

> To fall downe backwarde, of a wanton pevyshnes,
> Is non of those wayes, that God ever taught doughtles.
> Then if I ded it, I shuld tempt God very sore,
> And deserve to have, hys anger evermore.
>
> .   .   .   .
>
> For it is written, in the sext of Deuteronomy,
> Thu shalt in no wyse, tempt God presumptously.

But the episode is not over until his Jesus has been allowed to
expand the Deuteronomic text in a way that makes modern sense:

> Satan tentator.
> What is it to tempt God: after your judgement[?
> Jesus Christus.
> To take of hys worde, an outwarde experyment.

By this time Bale's Satan has lost both plausibility and momentum. He dourly leads Christ to the mountain and offers him all the resources of all the kingdoms of the world; but in contrast to Milton's poem, there is no grandeur on display. Bale's Satan merely lists the standard objects of worldly desire. With the temptations in this order, Bale cannot capitalize on the idea of a Satan who learns from experience to use the Word against the Word. Consequently, what we have is *dejà lu*. The motivation for Jesus Christus to accept his offer, Bale's Satan suggests, must be once again to distrust the God who leaves him so entirely without resources, and to turn that distrust against the heavenly message that started the confrontation:

> Forsake the beleve, that ye have in Gods worde,
> That ye are hys sonne, for it is not worth a torde

The disgraceful rhyming of God's 'worde' with 'torde' (piece of dung) is fine comedic shock, more definite than the half- or feminine rhymes that follow:

Loke on these kyngdomes, and incomparable treasure.
I the lorde of them, may geve them at my pleasure.
Forsake that father, whych leveth the without confort,
In thys desolacyon, and hens fourth to me resort.
Knowledge me for head, of thys worlde unyversall.
And I wyll make the, possessor of them all.
Thou shalt no longar, be desolate and hungrye,
But have all the worlde, to do the obsequye.
Therfor knele down here, and worshypp me thys houre,
And thu shalt have all, with their whole strength and poure.

By now we should know what to expect from this conversation:

> Jesus Christus.
> Avoyde thu Sathan, Thu devyll, thu adversarye,
> For now thu perswadest most damnable blasphemye.
>
> .   .   .   .
>
> For it is written, in the tenth of Deuteronomye,
> God thu shalt worshypp, and magnyfye alone.

This is the third time that Bale's Jesus has explicitly invoked Deuteronomy in a scholarly manner; and here his reference is to Chapter 10: 20, only one of several such injunctions that punctuate the delivery of the Ten Commandments.

Now, the dramatic conclusion: in Bale's play, muttering his threats, Satan departs, and the first and second Angels come and bring Christ food. Matthew has no such scene. For this purpose, Bale needed to switch to Luke's account. The angels then define the great generosity of the incarnation, and address the audience directly.

> Angelus Primus. *Plebem alloquitur.*
> The lorde here for yow, was borne and circumcysed,
> For yow here also, he was lately baptysed,
> In the wyldernesse, thys lorde for yow hath fasted,
> For yow hath overcomen, for you the devyll that tempted.
> For yow fryndes for yow, thys heavenly lorde doth all,
> Only for your sake, he is become man mortall.
> *Hic dulce canticum coram Christo depromunt.* ['Here they perform a sweet song in the presence of Christ.']

In neither Matthew nor Luke is there any mention of angelic song; but in Milton 'Angelic Choirs | Sung Heavenly Anthems of his victory', for about 45 lines, to which we shall return.

The *Temptacyon of Christ* ends with the return of 'Balus Prolocutor', who punches home the message about reliance solely on Scripture, in five stanzas of rhyme royal. Naturally he is concerned that Protestants should have access to Scripture. 'What enemyes are they that from the people will [remove] | The scriptures of God ... They brynge in fastinge, but they leave out Scriptum est.' Bale was responding to the efforts of Bishop Stokesley and others in the 1530s to suppress Tyndale's and Coverdale's bibles, an effort underwritten by royal proclamation in 1546.

In 1673, a year after the publication of *Paradise Regained*, Milton still found it necessary, in *Of True Religion*, to remind everybody that access to the Scriptures is a central tenet of Protestantism: 'The Papal Antichristian Church permits not her Laity to read the Bible in their own tongue: Our Church on the contrary hath proposed it to all men, and to this end translated it into English' (*CPW* 8: 434). But by this time his commitment to a Protestant exegesis of the Temptation had been overtaken by other concerns.

The problem of the threefold test of folklore, for someone not embedded in its culture, is in understanding why the final test *is* the final test. Why is it harder than the two that precede it? Now if Bale had used the order in Luke, the debate on the principles of scriptural citation would have come as the intellectual climax. Using the Matthew order, Bale had no more advanced *conceptual* move to make. Milton, however, saw what Luke saw—that the answer to the temptation on the pinnacle deserves its final position because it deals with Satan's newly learned debater's move. Recourse to Scripture is to be answered by Scripture itself. But, if Milton knew Bale's play, it is rather significant that he chooses to ignore the theological question of what constitutes misuse of Scripture, and instead opts for absolute brevity, a technique that is even more devastating to his Adversary.

I hope that I have demonstrated that Milton knew Bale's interlude and learned a good deal from it, including the structural advantage of using the order as in Luke. Both emphasize and extend the thought of a festive conclusion as in Matthew. Both Bale and Milton believe that the Temptation is essentially about reliance on the word of God, as relayed with supreme force at moments in the Mosaic books, and as heard again direct from heaven at the moment of the Baptism. Both accept the causal theory that it was the announcement of Jesus' divinity at the Baptism that alerted Satan to imminent danger.

Yet there are, obviously, vast differences in tone, in length, in emphasis. Bale is more worried by the special problems of how Scripture is to be used. Milton's Jesus does not engage in a discussion as to what it might mean to tempt God, but rebuffs Satan with absolute economy. 'Also it is written, | Tempt not the Lord thy God; he said and stood' (*PR* 4: 560–61). This conclusion has dazzled Milton's readers in its denial of argument and demonstration. Yet *Paradise Regained* is overall much less economical than Bale's play. What it saves on the roundabouts it lavishes on the swings. It has, to put it simply, many more words, and though it argues for simplicity, it does not, except in the rebuttal of the last temptation, exhibit it. What are we to make of this?

This brings us to the question of genre. The poem *now* presents itself with all the signs that it was intended as a sequel to *Paradise Lost*; at least by comparison with *Paradise Lost* it is brief; and, given its allusions to the Book of Job, it is inevitably linked back to Milton's statement in *Reason of Church Government* that there was such a genre as a brief epic, of which the Book of Job was the primary, if not the only, example. Barbara Lewalski's *Milton's Brief Epic*, which itself was far from brief, seemed to settle the matter once and for all.

Two years after the appearance of Lewalski's study, however, it was still possible for William Riley Parker, in his biography of Milton, to regard this thesis as a 'temptation', and to observe that by 'Milton's pupil, Edward Phillips, and by many other contemporaries the Book of Job was considered to be drama'. It was also Parker who observed that three-quarters of *Paradise Regained* consists of speeches, either dialogue, address, or formal soliloquy, and that the remaining quarter was probably composed and dictated between 1665 (the time when young Thomas Ellwood had his conversation with Milton about the missing follow-up to *Paradise Lost*) and July 2, 1670, when the poem was licensed for publication by Thomas Tomkyns (pp. 616–17).

Ellwood had worked with Milton for some months, reading aloud to the blind poet in return for instruction in Latin. Later he recorded in his journal a visit to Milton in June 1665, in which he was handed a bulky manuscript—the manuscript of *Paradise Lost*—and invited to read it and comment upon it. The comment he tells us he made has become legend: 'Thou has said much here of paradise lost, but what hast thou to say of paradise found?' The impertinent question was followed by a long, pregnant silence.

Later, though, alas, without specifying a date, Ellwood tells us that Milton handed him a copy of *Paradise Regained*, with a generous comment: 'This is owing to you, for you put it into my head by the question you put to me at Chalfont, which before I had not thought of.' Parker concluded that Milton had in his possession *'an unfinished drama* on "Christ's Victory and Triumph"... or "The Temptation of Christ"' (p. 616; italics added), which he was able to expand as needed.

Perhaps *Paradise Regained* was indeed begun as a drama, perhaps under the influence of Bale, and only converted to being the sequel to *Paradise Lost* on the basis of Ellwood's provocation. The text as produced by both Matthew and Luke was *already* dramatic in structure. The rhetorical exchange between the Son and the Tempter had been a subject of at least three medieval mystery plays, not counting Bale's. Perhaps Milton had sketched out a Temptation play during the period of his early fascination with drama, the period that begins with *Comus* and leads to the long, long list of plans and sketches for drama that he inscribed in the Trinity manuscript—a list that, to be honest, does not include the Temptation. On the other hand, perhaps that list does not include a Temptation play precisely because Milton had already roughed one out in manuscript.

When Ellwood years later arrived with his slightly tactless question, it would have been relatively easy for Milton to change the genre of an old, *Comus*-like, talky, Temptation play (an interesting companion to *Samson Agonistes*) by adding the narrative equivalent of speech-prefixes. Usually these consist of a single, barely functional line. I quote a few of them:

> To whom our Saviour sternly thus replied.
> To whom our Saviour with unaltered brow.
> To whom quick answer Satan thus returned.
> To whom thus Jesus, what conclud'st thou hence?
> To whom the Tempter murmuring thus replied.
> To whom the Fiend with fear abashed replied.
> To whom the Fiend now swoll'n with rage replied.

There are twenty of these undistinguished markers, and the poem would be better without them. As a stylistic tic, 'To whom' compares unfavorably with the strategic 'He who' of the prose tracts; anybody, even a secretary, could have written these lines.

If this hypothesis has any merit, we need to ask what Milton's revisions accomplished. Is the product improved? Is it coherent? For of course it is not only the speech-prefixes that would have been added, but also the narrative links and passages of description—the formal signs of epic. Some of these 'additions' seem to hark back to Milton's earlier literary hopes and plans, or might even be fragments of earlier projects, as in the banquet scene (structurally unnecessary since Jesus has *already* dismissed the temptation to change stones into bread) or the vision of the world in arms that he is shown in Book 3. Both of these adduce analogies to the romances that Milton had read for narrative inspiration in his youth, the Arthurian tales or the Carolingian ones. And then, as if to acknowledge the charge that I am making, Milton makes a joke:

> So saying [Satan] caught him up, and without wing
> Of Hippogrif bore through the Air sublime
> Over the Wilderness ...   (*PR* 4: 541–43)

His Satan doesn't need the memorable winged beast of Arios-
to's *Orlando Furioso* to carry his hero, because he himself is
twice as marvellous; once, in the invention of the gospellers
(though neither Matthew nor Luke actually mention flight); and
again, in Milton's fixation, ever since the 'Vacation Exercise', on
what words can do. They can make you think you can fly.

Without wing of Hippogrif? This is the denial that gives the
game away. As *Paradise Regained* yearns backwards in language, and exhibits the allure of the old stories of heroism, it
defeats itself. It becomes a poem divided between two irrecon-
cilable ideas of the word, of what is written—the most fundamental, both minimalist and true, and the most baroque. The
more Milton puts into it, the more, you will say, there is for the
Son to discard. But it is not just Satan who represents self-
indulgent copiousness. The author has to bear some responsi-
bility. Even the rejection of non-biblical writing—the praise of
'our native Language' that Jesus, the Jew, adduces as a reason to
reject classical learning and philosophy—goes on too long.
Some of us will wish, eighty lines later, that he had stopped
after that great Miltonic negative chiasmus:

> Think not that I know these things; or think
> I know them not.   (4: 286–87)

And some of what Milton added cannot even be explained by
the notion that it provided more for the Son to reject. *After* the
stern simplicity of the third rejection, Milton expanded considerably on his sources. First, there is a twenty-line statement
(plumped out by not one but two classical similes) that Satan

'fell', of which 'fact' there is no trace in the gospels. The word 'fell' or 'fall' is here repeated five times—with manifest theological intentions. Then Milton expands, for twelve lines, on Matthew's one-sentence report that the angels came and ministered to him; and for forty lines on Bale's modest invention of the angelic song. Indeed, Bale's angels sing to the audience, but Milton's sing first to the Son, and then to Satan. Lecture would be a better word. Bale's angels speak only of the gospel life of Christ, and his sacrifice. Milton's tell the whole story of Christianity (as revised by himself) from the creation of the Son through his victory over Satan in the war in heaven, thereby inserting Milton's own heretical Christology, with its Socinian tendencies. Was this desire to improve on his sources Milton's last and greatest temptation? Did he think he was rewriting Scripture?

In its final passages, *Paradise Regained* makes clear what a heretical text it really is, consistent with Milton's increasing fascination with Socinianism, and its belief that the Crucifixion, with its melodramatic cruelty of the son sacrificed by or to the father, could not really be the center of Christianity. Socianianism—to greatly oversimplify—struggled to make Jesus less divine, more fully human than Catholic and even mainstream Protestant theology would allow. For Milton, it was by passing the *intellectual* tests—by surviving the Temptation in the Wilderness—that Jesus redeemed us from the Fall of Adam, and at the end of the poem he has a chorus of angels descend, rescue Jesus from the pinnacle of the Temple, bring him food, and explain it to him properly. 'Now', they sing, 'thou hast aveng'd | Supplanted Adam, and vanquishing | Temptation, hast regain'd lost Paradise.' Not you will, but you already have. And their last words are these: 'Now enter, and begin to save mankind.' At first, I was stymied by the contradiction between these two statements; but now I see that they not only complete the word series on 'begin' that holds the poem together, but they explain the nature of the mission. It would be by his 'sayings'— by teaching an entirely new and austere and demanding code of ethics—that the perfect man promoted a better world.

Rude Words

Despite the return to general admiration for, even wonder at, Milton's brilliant way with words, there is one aspect of his lexicon that still shadows his revaluation. This is abuse. Some of Milton's most forceful language is unpleasant, not to say revolting. It was part of the apprenticeship that he served by becoming a polemicist, but he did not exactly grow out of it, not, at least, until he had finally embarrassed himself. In the English prose pamphlets we can recognize it as what used to be called billingsgate but might now be renamed trash talk. Its resources, not surprisingly, are plain words of native origin such as *foot, wen, big toe, snout, stench*, and *jakes*, all rather Shakespearean. In his Latin pamphlets he would fall back on more learned-sounding equivalents, *inquinamenta* (filth), *sterquilinium* (dung heap), or *acerbitatis evomere* (to vomit gall).

The genre of polemic assumed the use of fighting words, and Milton took care to justify his nastiness in terms of biblical precedent. The most obscene of his pamphlets are *Of Reformation*, *Animadversions*, and *Colasterion*, all of which are early work in this genre. But Milton was still flinging rude remarks and debasing, rather than debating, his opponent in the

Defenses, where, because we usually read them in translation, some of the worst graffiti have been partially sponged away. We cannot allow ourselves to avert our eyes from this aspect of Milton's talent. He could wield scurrility with as much flair as he could raise his reader's aspirations.

The Bishop's Foot

Let us start with *A Postscript*, because that is where, apparently, Milton started his career in prose. *A Postscript* was attached to *An Answer to a Booke, Entituled, An Humble Remonstrance*, the Presbyterian response to Bishop Joseph Hall's defense of episcopacy. The *Answer* was itself written by a committee of Presbyterian divines, under leadership of Thomas Young, Milton's old teacher. The *Postscript* was just under nine pages, and consisted largely of historical proofs of the insidious effect of episcopacy in England, those proofs being taken from the same editions of Holinshed, Speed, and Stow that Milton had cited in the Commonplace Book. Five of the references to Holinshed are identical with those in the Commonplace Book. But it has also been proved by W. T. Hale that there is a close connection between the *Postscript* and the first of Milton's church reform pamphlets, *Of Reformation*, so close that it is now assumed that the author of the *Postscript* was also Milton. This makes *A Postscript* his first entry into the polemical fray, an entry sheltered by anonymity and, presumably, the approval of Thomas Young. In its conclusion, the *Postscript* summarizes the contributions of the English episcopate since the reign of Elizabeth:

For it has beene their great designe to hinder all further
reformation; to bring in doctrines of Popery, Arminia-
nisme, and Libertinisme, to maintaine, propagate
and much increase the burden of humane ceremonies:
to keepe out and beate downe the Preaching of the
Word... And to tread downe the power of godlinesse.
Insomuch as it is come to an ordinary Proverb, that
when any thing is spoyled wee use to say, The Bishops
foot hath beene in it. And in all this... fulfilling Bishop
Bonners Prophesie, who when he saw that in King
Edwards reformation, there was a reservation of ceremonies and Hierarchy, is credibly reported to have used
these words; Since they have begun to tast of our Broath,
it will not be long ere they will eat of our Beefe.

(*CPW* 1: 975)

The *Answer* appeared on March 20, 1641. *Of Reformation*
appeared (also anonymously) in late May or early June. In
July Milton published *Animadversions*, a mock-dialogue with
the Remonstrant (Hall). The last section of this tract is subtitled
'To the Postscript', in which Milton virtually acknowledged his
authorship of it (though since *Animadversions* was itself anonymous, this clue led nowhere). Because Hall, in his *Defence of
the humble Remonstrance*, had made the mistake of bringing
up the 'bishop's foot' and Bonner's broth, and had suggested
that the author of the *Postscript* had spoiled the otherwise
decorous *Answer*, Milton took the opportunity to spit back:

Spoyld quoth ye? Indeed it is so spoyld, as a good song is
spoyld by a lewed singer, of as the saying is, God sends

meat, but the cooks worke their wills; in that sense we grant your Bishops foot may have spoyled it, and made Sapere ollam [smell of the pot], if not Sapere aulam [smell of Hall], which is the same in old Latin, and perhaps in plaine English. For certain your confutation hath atchiev'd nothing against it, and left nothing upon it, but a foule taste of your skillet foot, and a more perfect and distinguishable odour of your socks, then of your night-cap. And how the Bishop should confute a book with his foot, unless his braines were dropt into his great toe, I cannot meet with any man that can resolve me, onely they tell me that certainly such a confutation must be goutie. So much for the Bishops foot.   (*CPW* 2: 733)

An 'ordinary Proverb' and 'plaine English' of the most vulgar sort are now what Milton digs out of the coffer of his native language for his first venture into polemic. As for Bonner's broth, which the puppet Remonstrant in the margin is forced to recall:

The broth was your owne, you have been inviting the Land to it this four-score years, and so long we have been your slaves to serve it up for you, much against our wils, we know you have the Beefe to it, ready in your Kitchins, we are sure it was almost sod before this Parliament begun; what direction you have given since your Cooks to set it by in the Pantry till some fitter time, we know not, and therefore your deare jest is lost.

It takes an editor's note to fill out Milton's 'deare jest', that Bonner's broth is the blood of the martyrs who died in the Marian persecution.

Latin puns, smelly socks, brains dashed out, gouty feet, and implied cannibalism. There is almost too much going on here, too fast, for the reader to take it all in, though the general effect must be distaste. And Milton could not let this one go. In *An Apology against a Pamphlet*, the last of the church reform pamphlets, he returned to the metaphor of prelatical feet in smelly socks, suggesting that a bishop's foot with a linen sock over it 'is the aptest emblem of the Prelate himself... and sends a fouler stench to heaven, then that which this young queasinesse reches at' (*CPW* 2: 894). But now this stale joke is invoked in order to justify his use of such low style by biblical precedent: 'I beseech ye friends,... resolve me and your selves, is it blasphemy, or any whit disagreeing from Christian meeknesse, when as Christ himself speaking of unsavory traditions, scruples not to name the Dunghill and the Jakes' (895). Shortly afterwards he objects to translations or glosses that cover up obscenity in Scripture:

> Fools who would teach men to read more decently then God thought good to write. And thus I take it to be manifest, that indignation against men and their actions notoriously bad, hath leave and authority oft times to utter such words and phrases as in common talke were not so mannerly to use... all words and whatsoever may be spoken shall at some time in an unwonted manner wait upon her purposes.   (*CPW* 2: 903)

I suggest that a great deal of Milton's verbal energy in the church reform pamphlets derives from his unknowing obsession with the body, or the lower parts of it, and that breaking stylistic taboos allowed him to be incredibly inventive in the to-and-fro of pamphlet warfare. It is, of course, the theme of *Of Reformation* that the English church has retained the 'fleshly' habits of Roman Catholicism, in retaining its ceremonies, vestments, and physical signs of spiritual ideas. Milton calls this 'the new vomited Paganisme', and there is a good deal of vomit in his prose. He complains that, after the failure of the Wycliffite reformation, 'then was the Priest set to con his motions, and his Postures his Liturgies, and his Lurries' (*CPW* 2: 521–22) a phrase which includes two gross puns, since 'motions' could then mean bowel movements, and 'lurries' could mean diarrhea. Attacking the high Anglican preference for altars, he sneers, the communion table 'now becomes a Table of separation . . . to keep off the profane touch of the Laicks, whilst the obscene and surfeited Priest scruples not to paw, and mammock the sacramental bread, as familiarly his Tavern Bisket' (548). In *Animadversions*, much of which is provoked by the Anglican liturgy, and is hence an argument over fit words, he compliments his opponent thus: 'You do well to be the Sewer of your owne messe' (667). Hall's claim that the liturgy was written so as to allow as many Catholics as possible to join the national church he compares to 'the desire of Tamar, who to raise up seed to her Husband sate in the common road drest like a Curtezan, and he that came to her committed incest with her' (688–89). Clerical livings are 'the very garbage that drawes together all the fowles of prey and ravin in the land to come, and gorge upon the Church' (718); 'And let not those wretched Fathers thinke they shall impoverish the Church of willing, and able supply, though they keep back their sordid sperm begotten in the lustinesse of their avarice...rather let them take heed what lessons they instill into that lump of flesh which they are the cause of' (722). At the end of the *Apology* Milton descends to talking about farts: 'they have also this guift,...to have their voice in their bellies, which being well drain'd and taken down, their great Oracle, which is only there, will soone be dumbe' (953). These are the tactics that link Milton both backward to the Marprelate pamphlets of the Elizabethan era of struggle over church government and forward to Andrew Marvell's *Rehearsal Transpros'd*. But the Marprelate pamphlets were not quite this rude, and were genuinely funny. And Marvell, much though he learned from Milton, more quickly became disgusted by this style of debate; his last words against Samuel Parker were 'I have spit out your dirty Shoon'.

The King's Wen

As an emblem of Milton's strategy in these early pamphlets we can set up his giant Wen, which forms a visual center for *Of Reformation*. A wen is most simply a wart, but pathologically 'a sebaceous cystic tumour under the skin, occurring chiefly on the head'. Earlier in *Of Reformation* he had exclaimed: 'Alas Sir! A Commonwealth ought to be but as one huge Christian personage, one mighty growth and stature of an honest man' (*CPW* 2: 572). Today's readers will immediately think of the famous frontispiece to Hobbes's *Leviathan*, which was not, of course, yet published. Milton's is an ideal formulation, Hobbes's a pragmatic one. But a few pages later Milton revisits this giant in cartoon fashion, by reviving the fable of the Body and the Members as told in Livy and in Shakespeare's *Coriolanus*. In Milton's version, though he has complained bitterly about the well-fed bellies of the bishops, the theme of this fable is not the distribution of food, but status:

> Upon a time the Body summon'd all the Members to meet in the Guild for the common good (as Æsops Chronicles averre many stranger Accidents) the head by right takes the first seat, and next to it a huge and monstrous Wen little lesse then the Head it selfe, growing to it by a narrower excrescency. The members amaz'd began to aske one another what hee was that took place next their chief; none could resolve. Whereat the Wen, though unweildy, with much adoe gets up and bespeaks the Assembly to this purpose. That as in place he was second to the head, so by due of merit; therefore hee thought it for the honour of the Body, that such dignities and rich indowments should be decreed him, as did adorne, and set out the noblest Members.   (*CPW* 1: 584)

The Head, of course, signified the monarch; the Members, probably, both houses of parliament. The Wen—a good old Anglo-Saxon word if ever there was one—stood for all the bishops in the kingdom. Its claim to 'dignities and rich indowments' represented the church's claim to lands, living, tithes, etc.—all the emoluments against which Milton would still be arguing in 1659, in *Likeliest means to remove Hirelings out of the church*. To simplify his message, Milton has to build into his fable an internal interpreter, 'a wise and learned Philosopher', who is given the charge of evaluating the Wen's claims as a one-man parliamentary committee. 'Wondring at the boldnesse of such a swolne Tumor, Wilt thou (quoth he) that art but a bottle of vitious and harden'd excrements, contend with the lawfull and free-borne members, whose certaine number is set by ancient and unrepealable Statute?' The Wen then makes the incredible claim that the Soul needs this excrescence as a place to retire 'from over the steaming vapours of the lower parts, to Divine Contemplation, with him shee found the purest, and quietest retreat, as being most remote from soile, and disturbance'. Milton was stretching the skin of the fable way past its normal extension. We cannot help being relieved when the Philosopher cuts the conversation short. The Wen, he says, is nothing but a 'heape of hard, and loathsome uncleannes', whose contents will shortly be revealed by lancing and surgical excision.

The revised fable is a tour de force. The over-excitement that emanates from these pamphlets is a symptom of a great talent discovering itself, by primarily negative and destructive means. Towards the end of the *Apology*, Milton notes a partial compliment that Hall has paid him: '*such a volley of expressions* he hath met withal, *as he would never desire to have them better cloth'd*'. Preening, Milton, presents himself as one 'whose mind so ever is fully possest with a fervent desire to know good things, and with the dearest charity to infuse the knowledge of them into others, when such a man would speak, his words (by what I can expresse) like so many nimble and airy servitors trip about him at command, and in well order'd files, as he would wish, fall aptly into their own places' (*CPW* 1: 948–49). By the time he has written the *Defenses* and the *Pro se Defensio*, he will not be so complacent. Meanwhile, the 'steaming vapours of the lower parts' would, as we have seen, reappear in another context in his next major project, the *Doctrine and Discipline of Divorce*.

But if the *Doctrine* was obsessed, perhaps understandably, with those parts of the body that are involved in sexual intercourse, *Colasterion*, Milton's last pamphlet on divorce, shows how much lower he can sink, linguistically. For here we find not periphrasis, but gutter talk. He justifies this descent to the lowest of the styles by suggesting that his opponent is a 'serving man', turned lawyer. Milton assumes that low social status justifies being called 'a Boar in a Vinyard', or a Barrow (hog) that can only grunt at the phrase 'gentle breeding' (*CPW* 2: 751), who 'leaves the noysom stench of his rude slot behind him' (751). 'But what should a man say more to a snout in this pickle, what language can be low and degenerat anough' (747). Bathroom language, evidently. As for his 'friends and followers', Milton advises them to take the advice of *Colasterion's* author, 'to sit upon the stool and strain', until they can overcome their dislike of their spouses (738).

The Cock and the Hen

There is little satisfaction to be gained by reading the *First Defense of the English People*. Being given the task of rebutting the *Defensio Regia, Pro Carola I* by Claude de Saumaise (Salmasius) was certainly an honor for Milton, and it should not have been too strenuous a task, even though he approached it with damaged eyes. He had already worked out the central arguments for the regicide in the *Tenure*, and he had merely to follow the accepted method of animadversions, whereby one takes the assertions of one's adversary serially, and disproves or discredits them. The organization, therefore, of the pamphlet was already in place. There was, however, a problem with words. As Milton remarked in his Preface, 'If I be as copious of words and empty of matter (*tam sim profusus verborum, vacuus rerum*) as most men think Salmasius has been in his Defence of the King, I fear that I shall apparently have deserved to be called a defender at once wordy and silly (*verbosissimi simul et ineptissimi defensoris*) (*CE* 7: 2–3). The fluency on which he had congratulated himself in writing the church reform pamphlets might now become a liability, especially since he had to follow where Salmasius led and overwhelm him with other and better authorities. And, of course, Milton was now to put his Latinity to the test before an international audience, while mocking that of his adversary.

The fact is that Milton's 'native language', invoked in the *Vacation Exercise* as capable of great subjects, was better suited to smart repartee than Latin, which was not good at hyperbole. We soon become suspicious of those 'issimus' extensions, which Samuel Wolff, the translator for the Columbia edition, has already decided to ignore. The vocabulary of classical Latin, being frozen in time, was small compared to English, equipped as it was with its own Latinisms to contrast with pungent 'native' words. And the range or quality of insults had not improved since antiquity. The nastiest tool in Milton's arsenal, not unconnected to the divorce pamphlets, was the rumor that Salmasius was a henpecked husband; and he had also heard that

Salmasius had received a hundred gold coins from Charles II for
his services as propagandist. Let us see what Milton does with
this. I cite Wolfe's translation, which makes the best of a bad
business:

> '*Gallus gallinaceus*, the cock', you say, 'wields imperial
> power over both males and females.' How can that be,
> since you yourself that are Gallic, and (they say) but too
> cocky, wield not imperial power over your hen, but she
> over you? So that if the gallinaceous cock be king over
> many females, you that are slave to your hen must needs
> be not Gallus gallinaceous, but some sort of Gallus
> stercorarius, or dunghill-cock. For the matter of books,
> in fact, nobody publishes huger dunghills, and you
> deafen us all with your crowing over them; that is the
> only point in which you resemble a true cock. I promise
> to give you many barley-corns if in ransacking this
> whole dunghill-book of yours you can shew me but
> one jewel. But why should I give barley to you, who,
> quite unlike the honest plain cock in Aesop, scratched
> not for barley, but like the good-for-nothing cock in
> Plautus, scratched eagerly for gold? The outcome, to be
> sure, was different to this extent, that by scratching you
> found a hundred gold Jacobuses . . .   (*CE* 7: 281)

Now it is true that Salmasius had handed Milton this opportunity by including the *Gallus gallinaceus* as an example of
natural rulers in the animal kingdom. He thereby invited the
pun on 'gallus', a Gaul or Frenchman, and the beast in question.
But Milton, knowing that classical authors had connected the

cock naturally with pride, lust, and dunghills, blended those standard aspects with Plautus' cock in *Aulularia* (ll. 465–71) and Aesop's fable of the cock who found a jewel in the dust, and composted the whole into a double-edged slur on Salmasius as writer and husband. Clever, but, we might also say, too cocky. Two words, *gallinaceus* and *sterquilinium*, each repeated more often than necessary, especially since the first already implied the second.

We need not belabor the point, just because Milton did. And although there are other insults scattered through the *First Defense*, and other unflattering identifications with beasts, the tract in general kept steadily to its task, to undermine the arguments for monarchy derived from law or natural law or Scripture or history or natural history, block by block. Milton remained proud of the *First Defense*. He had it published in a new edition in 1658. He believed that he had won the argument with Salmasius. But as always with Milton, a venture into a new genre engendered sequels. The *First Defense* led to the *Second*, the *Second* directly to the *Pro se Defensio*.

The *Second Defense* was a response to the *Regia Sanguinis Clamor*, the *Cry of the royal blood* against the regicides, which appeared in 1652 and whose author Milton believed, erroneously, to be Alexander More, professor of church history in Amsterdam, and a friend of Salmasius. More was in fact not the author, but he was responsible for putting the *Cry* through the press, and had written the prefatory epistle to Charles II which insulted Milton and his blindness. Although Milton had been warned that More was not the author, he wrote the *Second Defense* attacking him personally, as the *Cry* had indeed personally attacked him. Milton wrote the *Second Defense* at the top of his voice, and was less concerned to defend the king's execution theoretically than to defend himself and to raise the revolution to epic status. Once again, the sex life of his assumed adversary was made fair game, more fair at any rate than his mockery of Salmasius, since More had seduced and abandoned a female attendant of Salmasius' wife; but the passages of insult and scandal are today overlooked in favor of Milton's massive eulogy to Oliver Cromwell, one way of dealing with the uncomfortable fact that Cromwell's Protectorate had replaced the republic Milton had argued for, which did not bode well for Milton's values. During the *Defense* Milton provided his readers with the longest account yet of his own life and work, giving only the most idealistic account of his motives. 'I have delivered my testimony', he wrote, 'I might almost say I have erected a monument that will not readily be destroyed.' Unfortunately there was still one more defense to come.

The Upupa

In October 1654 the publisher of the *Cry*, Adriaan Vlacq, provoked another phase of the quarrel. Alexander More had partially written a defense of himself, the *Fides Publica*, which Vlacq proceeded to publish in its unfinished form as a pendant to a second, unauthorized *Second Defense*, one of three pirated and badly printed editions. So Milton was publicly yoked to the man of whom, quite without warrant, he had made a personal enemy. In *Fides Publica*, More denied authorship of the *Cry*, and indeed accused Milton of having already been informed he was not the author before the *Second Defense* was published. That is, he accused him of slander; but not only of slander, since having suspected his error, Milton was unwilling, More suggests, to waste all his work, to forgo all those puns on his name, Morus, the Fool. Shrewdly, More suggests that defense of 'the people' is only a pretext: 'as often as you speak for the people your language grows weak, becomes feeble...as often as you speak for yourself, which you do oftener than not the whole thing swells up, ignites, burns'. And worse still, he panders to the lowest of his readers:

> No merchandise is more vendible, none induces a more eager buyer, than an abusive and wanton book, whose words enter the loins of youth, as you would say, and teach the vileness which you relate. Moreover these elements make a strange appeal to the common people, so that to me you would seem to have written not only for the people, but to the people.
>
> (*Fides Publica*, tr. Paul Blackford; *CPW* 4: 2: 1108)

There is little doubt that Milton had a guilty conscience when he began the *Pro se Defensio*, and an even guiltier one when he completed it.

As he had in the *Apology*, Milton responds again to the charge of indecency by blaming the target:

> 'I promised the ambassador', you say, that 'nothing indecorous should issue from my pen.' I have not failed that promise; or if I have done aught in that respect,

> I have done an injustice upon myself alone, when I took
> upon myself the task of examining your putridity and
> discussing your filth (*inquinamenta*).   (*CPW* 4: 2: 743)

More has accused him of using 'verbis nudis & praetextatis',
'words naked and unchaste'. 'But what phrase, what word will
you show me in the whole book fouler than the name of
Morus?' This was an unfortunate move, since More's name
should never have appeared in the *Second Defense*. But Milton
then proceeds to defend himself by claiming that 'gravest
authors' have always thought that 'words unchaste and plain
thrust out with indignation signify not obscenity, but the vehe-
mence of gravest censure'. And he lists Piso and Sallust, who
both mention the penis, Herodotus, Seneca, Suetonius, Plu-
tarch, 'the gravest authors of all', not to mention the Church
Fathers, Moses himself, and the prophets. How, one wonders,
did Milton arrive at this list? What other kind of commonplace
book had he kept?

One should really stop right there. But *Pro se Defensio* also
contains an Aesopian fable, broadly adapted. Towards the end
of the *Fides Publica*, More unwisely engages in the same exercise for which he had excoriated Milton—blowing his own
academic trumpet, supplying his scholarly credentials. So Milton plumes his imagination:

> A little crow steps forth, but it too is naked. Of a sudden
> it is so adorned with I know not how many fantastic
> plumes and borrowed colors that anyone might think it
> more like some kind of flamingo (*Phoenicopterus*)...
> You would declare the man had plucked the birds of

Aristophanes, but, if I am not much mistaken, under evil auspices. When he has been plucked, he will know that he is not now acting out a play, but demonstrating a fable of Aesop in his own person. For when I shall have shown, More, that those plumes are not your own, that they are partly decayed, and such as would have fallen off of their own accord, partly counterfeited with false colors, and partly stolen by trickery and witchcraft, there is no doubt that the flock of birds once deluded by you, having now discovered who you are, will take you to court for the restoration of their plumes, and when each has snatched back his own, you who were till now a phoenix, will be left at last a foul hoopoe (*upupa*), not only deplumed, but bare-buttocked.   (*CPW* 4: 2: 783–84)

The hoopoe had come down from antiquity with an ambivalent reputation. On the one hand, it was said that the young hoopoes cared for their aged parents, plucking out their old feathers to rejuvenate them; on the other, the bird was said by Pliny and Isidore of Seville to live on human excrement. Milton counts on his audience knowing the bird's nasty habits, and substitutes for the caring children the angry birds whose plumage has been stolen, paying the hoopoe back by denuding its backside. I doubt that Milton had ever seen a hoopoe, which in most of its variants is a beautiful bird, made more handsome by the erectile crest. Nor, it seems, had Paul Blackford, whose translation I cite, since his note mentions 'the obscene appearance' as well as 'the disgusting habits' of the hoopoe. It is now the national bird of Israel.

Collected like this, these fables seem to be a habit. They are, as it were, dark mirror images of the epic simile, whose ingenious expansion the reader is expected to admire. They serve as clusters of unpleasant words which, if thrown out separately, would seem random invective. But they do not solve the theoretical problem that Milton encountered when he moved from attacking a corporate body (the English bishops) or the formal representative of a system (monarchy) to a recognized (even commissioned) spokesman for that system (Salmasius) to a single man, and the wrong man at that.

In the preface to *Animadversions* Milton had defended a 'well heated fervencie' in polemic as justified by the fact that the souls of men were at stake. 'But they that seeke to discover and oppose their false trade of deceiving, do it not without a sad and unwilling anger, not without many hazards, but without all private and personall spleene' (*CPW* 1: 663). We now recognize as particularly Miltonic that 'not without' formula as a sign of writerly anxiety, and it was indeed a difficult task, especially in the genre of *Animadversions*, where one's adversary, though unnamed, is dragged in by the hair for endless rebuttal, to avoid the impression of 'private and personall spleene'. At the end of *Pro se Defensio* Milton virtually admits that he has failed in this rhetorical sleight of hand. His peroration is self-defensive in another sense than that which the tract's title implies. His last words are an extended hypothesis, rather than an assertion. The passage, which is all one long sentence, is so difficult and so important in its choice of words and syntax that I have chosen to translate it myself:

And *if* even from private enmities public transgressions are sometimes censured and often corrected, and *if* I have now, driven by all possible reasons, inflicted a most just censure on [someone] who is not only my personal enemy, but the enemy of almost the whole community, an execrable man, a disgrace to the reformed religion...whether with the appropriate success, let them see to it who are most interested in making an example of him, as for me I hope (for why should I doubt) that I have done a thing neither ungrateful to God, nor unhealthy for the church, nor without use to the Republic. (*CE* 9: 226)

Neque...ingratam...Neque...insalubrem...Neque inutilem. The negative syntax tells its own confessional story. (*Cur enim diffidam?*) Why indeed? Unless, as I suspect, Milton feared that for all his eloquent theoretical defense of abuse in a righteous cause, it is impossible to feel clean when talking dirty.

Negativity

'Worthy to have not remained so long unsung'

Several critics have noted that Milton tends to put his positives—his most important positives at that—in negative form. The above is an example. It comes from the formal opening, the statement of purpose, of *Paradise Regained*. It is one of the more twisted of Milton's claims for the importance of his poetic subjects, twisted in the grammatical sense. Its claims—to be at last singing the unsung—are, as we have seen, at least disingenuous. But its form is what concerns us here. The distorted syntax would have outraged F. R. Leavis, but in the larger context of how Milton learned to write it is fascinating.

My early hunch was that Milton learned to do this sort of thing from his deep familiarity with Latin syntax. Many negatives later, I concluded that not only was the hunch possibly correct, but that the discovery was far more interesting than I had dreamed. Far more can be learned from Milton's negativity, whether of syntax or of vocabulary, than what his lexical training had produced. He had an obsession with adjectives that are switched from a positive semantic register to a negative, or from a negative to a positive, by the use of the prefix un-, which is of course not Latinate but Anglo-Saxon. And when 'not' is included in the tangle, as in the example here, the reader's capacities for rapid comprehension are severely exercised.

Negative constructions begin early in Milton's poetry, and continue through his career as a prose polemicist. They become increasingly prevalent, and loaded with autobiographical freight, in the *Second Defense of the English People*, when Milton turns to defending himself; and in *Paradise Lost* they rise, if I might put it like this, to the level of the philosophical and theological. I put it like this because, since I first published these findings, I have read Kenneth Burke's thoughts on negativity and negative theology in *Language as Symbolic Action*, which, though somewhat unsystematic, have led me to sharpen my own thinking.

Let us begin with the young Milton, whose verbal habits or predilections were just beginning to become visible in *L'Allegro* and *Il Penseroso*, the companion poems that set out two alternative attitudes to life, the light-hearted and the grave. Milton puts himself in both poems, and connects these cameo appearances by echo:

> Missing thee, I walk **unseen**
> On the dry smooth-shaven Green.

and:

> Some time walking **not unseen**
> By Hedgerow Elms, on Hillocks green.

Unseen and not unseen. Small words, easily lost in the rich texture of poems whose texture consists of the pleasures of seeing as well as listening, both pleasures conveyed to readers through their own senses. Why would Milton choose these matched words to describe his own persona in morning and evening moods? Why not 'Missing thee, I walk obscure, | By the silver fountains pure', or 'Sometime walking in plain view, | Where congregates the rural crew?' *Il Penseroso*, it is true, thematizes invisibility by choice. The speaker walks 'in close covert by some Brook, | Where no profaner eye may look', and asks Night to 'hide [him] from Day's garish eye'. But why, in the lighter, seemingly simpler poem, would he see himself as 'sometime walking *not unseen*', a weird double negative so gratuitous, especially in its discovered echo in *Il Penseroso*, that it jolts us into rethinking the 'unreproved pleasures' of the poem, where the negative implies not freedom but the brooding presence of a figure of reproof.

Kenneth Burke begins his remarks on negativity by alluding, fortuitously for us, to the *De Doctrina Christiana*, not Milton's, but Augustine's, and alluding to Augustine's account of the three styles. 'We interpret the tenor of these remarks', writes Burke:

> to indicate that the grand style (and its secular equivalent, the poetically 'sublime'), operates in the regions of the *fearsome*, the 'negative' realm from which the idea of deterrence, of the thou-shalt-not, is never absent. (p. 454)

For Burke, this tendency of 'being essentially negative in the Decalogical way' is fundamental to language, and hence to human thought (at least in English). He goes so far as to suggest that where a theologian uses the term 'God' as the ultimate ground of thought, a secularist would instead use the word 'No' as the hard core of language, its ground.

> Thus, just as the 'ontological argument' for the existence
> of God proves itself out of itself, by saying that if there is
> being there must be perfect being, so our equivalent in
> linguistics would be our contention that *language by its*
> *nature necessarily culminates in the Negative, hence neg-*
> *ation is of the very essence of language.*   (p. 457)

As Burke corrects the theological approach to negative thinking by secularizing it, we will want to qualify his absolutist
rhetoric by appeal to other disciplines. Thus child psychology
can support the notion that the first word a child learns may be
'No' and so learns to extend the principle of 'No' into the whole
realm of commands, deterrents, motivations, and rewards.
Adult psychologies have long known, however, that some persons have a stronger *feeling* of the negative than others; from
Burton's *Anatomy of Melancholy* (which Milton read before
writing *L'Allegro* and *Il Penseroso*) to the modern discovery
that hope and despair can be modified by medicalization, we
have acknowledged that negativity may be inbuilt. And then
there is the hypothesis, the one with which I began, that the way
we are taught to write at an educated level may influence the
way our thoughts are capable of developing.

Let us now look at the learned habits of writing in Latin,
which Milton developed both early and to a degree unimagin-
able today. In *Ad Patrem*, the verse letter where Milton attempts
to persuade his father that a literary career will be worth his
costly education, he writes: 'Quae mihi sunt nullae, nisi quas
dedit aurea Clio' ('I have nothing except what golden Clio has
given'; l. 14). *Nullae ... nisi.* Not 'I have only Clio's golden gifts'.

And he writes: 'Nec tu vatis opus divinus despice carmen' ('Nor should you despise the divine song of the poet'; l. 17). *Nec... despice*. Why not, instead, 'You should honor the heavenly work'? And he writes: 'Nec tu perge, precor, sacras contemnere Musas, | Nec vanas inopesque puta' ('Do not persist, I beg of you, in condemning the sacred Muses, and do not think them vain and unuseful'; ll. 56–57). More of the same. *Nec... nec* and *inopes* instead of some other word that does not itself consist of a denial. And finally, should his appeal to his parent be successful, he looks forward to a different kind of life, one in which the values of *Il Penseroso* and *L'Allegro* somehow combine, at least as concerns his own place in the sight of others: 'Iamque nec obscurus populo miscebo inerti' ('I shall no longer mingle obscure with the unthinking rabble'). M. Y. Hughes here catches Milton's habit and translates *obscurus* as *unknown*. Milton is promising his father that he *will* be famous some day, and that the scrivener's investment in a university education will pay off. Something is going on here, and it is not too early to suggest that *Ad Patrem* is the visible site of Milton's vocational anxiety, the place where the problem of self-esteem emerges in the formulae that spring (unasked?) to his writing hand.

But this is only one strain of Milton's early negativity. There is another, primarily elegiac strain, already visible in the early poems. There is Lycidas, who 'must **not** float upon his wat'ry bier, | **Unwept**', a formula that alludes to the poet's responsibility for taking up neglected topics, and will return in fully theorized form in the invocation to *Paradise Lost*, Book 9. But there is also the purely pathetic and affective series of 'no mores', from the 'Willows and the Hazel Copses green' which shall 'now no more be seen', to 'Smite no more', 'Weep no more', and again, 'Weep no more'. And then there is one of the earliest of Milton's great divine paradoxes, 'the unexpressive nuptial song', which points to another theme, the inexpressibility of what matters most, and echoes the 'unexpressive notes' with which the angels in the *Nativity Ode* celebrate the birth of Christ (l. 116).

Before *Lycidas*, however, came *Comus*, or *A Masque*, which is tightly connected by a shared vocabulary to *L'Allegro* and *Il Penseroso*, but instead of a choice between two interesting alternatives is an exercise in denial. Philosophically, or ethically, the mandate of the masque is 'Just say no'. Or, more subtly, learn how to say 'no' without using the ground-word. Chastity and temperance are traditional terms for the same exercise, made dull by overuse. Milton is interested in having us feel the *force* of the negative by the accumulation of the un-principle, even in words where no ethical restraint is required.

The Lady, the center of the chastity test, is clearly La Penserosa. She has heard Comus' music as if it were the dance of 'loose unletter'd Hinds' (l. 174), and found herself in a world in which she doesn't know where to direct her 'unacquainted feet' (l. 180). Naturally she is worried about keeping her 'life and honour unassail'd' (l. 220). As for her brothers, their mouths are full of high-minded and high-class negatives, along with unnecessary ones. Among 'unnumerous boughs' (l. 349) they fear their sister 'leans her unpillow'd head' (l. 355). But, says the Elder Brother, *she* won't be anxious: 'I do not think my sister...so unprincipl'd in virtue's book...(Not being in danger, as I trust she is not)' (ll. 366–70). The Second Brother is a little less sanguine. Beauty needs a guardian dragon 'with unenchanted eye' (l. 395) to defend it. 'You may as well spread out the unsunn'd heaps | of Miser's treasure by an outlaw's den, | And tell me it is safe, as bid me hope | Danger will wink on Opportunity, | And let a single helpless maiden pass | Uninjured' (ll. 398–403) And his speech ends with the very odd phrase, 'our unowned Sister' (l. 407) which is no less disturbing for the legalistic gloss, 'not being possessed as property'.

Now, to make the point more strongly, I shall stop placing the negatives in context and simply list them as they fall, without line references: 'unblench't majesty', 'unlaid ghost', 'unconquered Virgin', 'unpolluted temple of the mind', 'unchaste looks', 'th'unwary sense of them that pass unweeting', 'th'unarmed weakness of one Virgin', 'unjust force', and, importantly, 'unknown' secretive herb Haemony. Half of these negatives have a negative point to make, the other half actually make positive statements. Comus does it too. He cites the 'unexempt condition of humanity', Nature's 'unwithdrawing hand', 'spawn innumerable', all arguments for using Nature's bounty, else 'Th'all giver would be unthank'd, would be unprais'd, | Nor half his riches known'. To which the Lady replies, using his strategy against him, that Nature would be better pleased if her goods were used 'in unsuperfluous even proportion'. Is this just a lexical habit run rampant, or is Milton trying to suggest that, when you are lost in the woods or in a long, argumentative poem, it is not always easy to distinguish a good negative from a bad one? The negative formations of the Elder Brother seem a bit too conventionally moral, those of

Comus a bit too obviously anti-conventional. Yet those of Comus have an insidious appeal, because they are more intelligent than simple *carpe diem*.

Thomas Corns has observed that Milton is more inventive in the *Masque* than in any other poem. That is to say, he invents more words. This makes sense for a young poet embarking on quite an important public commission, spreading his literary wings. Corns counted almost sixty coinages. He did not note, however, that many of these new words are negatives created by Milton for the purpose of the moment. Of the words listed above, 'unattending', 'unpillow'd', 'unenchanged', 'unblench't', 'unexempt', 'unwithdrawing', appear first in English here. 'Unnumerous' is not even registered in *OED*. 'Unowned' is used only by Milton in this figurative sense. And for 'unsunn'd', 'uninjured', 'unthank'd', and 'unsuperfluous' Milton is only the second user in each case. And we should not forget that in the *Masque* he is, for the first time, writing in blank verse, which demands a different kind of ornamentation from that which he had perfected in the *Nativity Ode*. This powerful combination of tools—blank verse and verbal innovation—would not come back into play until just before the Restoration. And when they did, years of experience in verbal combat would not only have increased Milton's lexical inventiveness, but also brought him a deeper understanding of what negativity might be and mean.

Now let's jump to the 1640s, and the period of Milton's English prose. Here is Milton's first account to the English public, that *populus inertus*, of his literary intentions. This is, of course, from the *Reason of Church Government*, published in January or February of 1642, and it speaks volumes about the intellectual (and syntactic) shape that Milton had now arrived at for the expression of what I earlier called writer's block. Given his willing embroilment in the cause of church reform as led by the Presbyterians, and the pleasure he discovered in verbal infighting, Milton invents a new language of vocational self-inspection. Here negativity is expressed not in coinages or adjectives turned against themselves by a negative prefix, but in syntax which plays grammatical negatives against each other, creating a psychological labyrinth:

> And the accomplishment of them lies **not but** in a power above mans to promise; but that **none hath with more studious ways** endeavour'd, and with more **unwearied** spirit that **none shall**, that I dare almost averre of my self. . . . **Neither do I think it shame** to covnant with any knowing reader, that for some few yeers yet I may go on trust with him toward the payment of what I am now indebted, as being a work **not to be rays'd** from the heat of youth or the vapours of wine, . . . **nor** to be obtain'd by the invocation of Dame Memory and her Siren daughters, but by devout prayer to that eternall Spirit . . . to this must be added industrious and select reading, steddy observation, insight into all seemly and generous arts and affairs, till which in some measure be compast, at mine own peril and cost **I refuse not** to sustain this expectation from as many **as are not loath to hazard so much credulity** upon the best pledges I can give them.   (*CPW* 1: 820–21)

If we translate this passage, and I think we must, not least because it is extremely difficult to do, what Milton is saying is roughly this:

> It is beyond human power to promise the accomplishment of my literary ambitions, but I almost dare swear that I have tried to do so by the most intense study (and I defy anybody to be more energetic than I have been). And I must confidently make a contract with any intelligent reader that what I have promised to produce will be available in a few more years, since it will not be the product of youthful enthusiasm or intoxication, nor arrived at by appealing to literary tradition, but rather the gift of the Holy Spirit; to which inspiration must be added industrious and select reading, steady observation [of the world], insight into all appropriate arts and affairs, and till this necessary preparation is completed, at my own peril and cost[,] I must continue to ask for patience and credibility from those who are willing to take the chance on me, on the basis of my best pledges.

But here's the twist. Does that anxious phrase, 'at mine own peril and cost', refer, as I have allowed it to by inserting a comma, to the costs of his literary apprenticeship (costs which, we may notice, are now his and not his father's); or does it, without the comma, reach forward to govern his refusal to be hurried, his statement that asking for more time is reasonable, given the quality of his credit? That the entire passage is shaped by the commercial metaphor of debt, delayed payment, and personal credit connects it both back to *Ad Patrem* and forward to the market metaphors of *Areopagitica*. Pledge, we might note, is a word which *could* be used in the sense of 'to give assurance of friendship or fidelity to any by the act of drinking', precisely that which Milton rejects, but also, more dramatically, 'to deliver, deposit, or assign as security for the repayment of a loan or the performance of some action'. What is Milton delivering? His eloquence only, his word, his most peculiar negative positivism.

We have now established a *mentalité* for Milton in which syntactical negativity is the sign of vocational doubt, the negative mirror image of his remarkable confidence. This discovery will need to be remade, again and again, in the three *Defenses*. But there is another aspect of Milton's work as a polemicist in which words are turned against themselves, as part of the mindset of public sparring. Thomas Corns is among the very few who has attended to the style of the early pamphlets and noted the frequency of pairs of negative adjectives, of which 'unexercis'd and unbreath'd' is the most famous example. But Corns only instances: 'Any ungenerous and unbeseeming motion' (*RCG* 1: 842) and 'Tyrannie unpraised or uncelebrated in a written monument' (*REW* 2, 7: 421), of which the second is highly misleading as cited here, since it is one of the many acts of self-congratulation that Milton engages in. To make sense, it should read 'our victory at once against two of the most prevailing usurpers over mankind, supersitition and tyrannie [,] unpraisd or uncelebrated'. 'Uncelebrated' is a coinage, by the way, which will reappear, along with its prior negation, in *Paradise Lost* (7: 253). Corns did not think that Milton combined more than two such terms in the prose works. But in fact

Milton, in *Of Reformation*, hoped to see the bishops 'undiocest, unrevenu'd, unlorded' (*CPW* 1: 549), in which every term is a coinage, and the whole sheer high spirits; so it is not quite true that 'the more developed version of the scheme, offering a certain flourish or finality, perhaps functions as a marker distinguishing the language of Miltonic poetic discourse' (Corns, p. 85). In fact, 'undiocest, unrevenue'd, unlorded' is a pentameter line with a feminine ending. *Tetrachordon* also offers us 'unconferred with, unadmonish'd, undealt with', and the wife who is 'unsociable, unpeacefull or unduteous' (*CPW* 2: 691), where 'unduteous' was Shakespeare's coinage, and the phrase is another pentameter triplet.

When we reach the divorce pamphlets, something more cerebral and brilliant is in motion. It stands to reason that the divorce pamphlets should offer a hoard of new negatives, both in single coinages and in phrases. There is the twice-used 'unaccomplishment' (*CPW* 2: 223 and 246); 'unconscionable' (2: 247); 'undelighted and in servile copulation', 'undelighted' being a coinage that will reappear in *Paradise Lost* as a descriptor of Satan's response to Eden; 'two incoherent and uncombining dispositions' (2: 270), where both words are coinages; and 'two persons unconjunctive, and unmariable together' (2: 328), where 'unmariable' does not even register in the *OED*. These rather striking instances are not just the results of Milton's negative feelings about his first marriage, but a strategy designed to come to terms with what Burke called 'the realm of the "thou-shalt-not" or "being essentially negative in the Decalogical way"'. Milton complains, as we know, that 'thou shalt not commit adultery' has had much too much prominence in the ethical theory of marriage', though 'by all the force of the Decalogue' the wife who belongs to another faith 'ought to be disbanded' (*CPW* 2: 260). But his main problem was not the Decalogue, the 'undispensing covenant' (2: 298) that Moses had made with the Jews. It was the Gospel. Moses had permitted divorce under certain much disputed conditions. Jesus had prohibited it absolutely. And Milton took this to be a 'hardheartednesse of undivorcing' (2: 311), a witty reversal of what is already a negative word. The claim of indissolubility is to be countered, verbally, by that of irreconcilability. And God himself, rather than his interpreters, 'lectures to us not only by those recited decrees, but ev'n by the first and last of all his visible works; when by his divorcing command the world first rose out of Chaos, not can be renew'd again out of confusion but by the separating of unmeet consorts' (2: 273).

Blindness

When Milton began to lose his eyesight, and especially after he became completely blind, the frustration so experienced results in a new use for the negativity of expression, and particularly of self-expression. If in *Comus* the flurry of negative constructions was appropriate to a poem whose central message is 'No', and if in the *Reason of Church Government* the negative syntax is clearly related to Milton's embarrassment at not having produced more than minor literary works, in the *Pro Populo Anglicano Defensio Secunda*, which Milton produced after his blindness was total, we can see both the embedded influence of

Latinity and the searing effects of privation. The former, of course, is the consequence of our *reading* the *Second Defense* in both Latin and English; the second is made visible because Milton rises to self-defense specifically on the issue of his blindness and what has caused it. Here the theme of being seen—how he looks in the eyes of others—is refocused on the question of how his now blind eyes look in the eyes of others. Let us start with an English translation, which is partly my own, partly that of the Columbia edition:

> No one, so far as I know, who has only seen me, has ever thought that I am deformed in appearance: whether handsome or not, is a point I shall less insist on. My stature, I own, is not tall...but it is not true, that I am thus lean beyond example; on the contrary [when I was younger]...I was neither unskilled in handling my sword, nor unpractised in its daily use...At this day, I have the same spirit, the same strength, [only] my eyes are not the same: yet to external appearance, they are undamaged, as clear and bright without a cloud, as the eyes of those whose sight is most perfect. In this respect only, and against my will, am I a dissembler. In my countenance, in which [my adversary] has said, there is 'nothing more bloodless', there still remains a color so very opposite to the bloodless and pale, that, though turned forty, there is scarcely anyone who would not think me younger by nearly ten years. Neither my body nor my skin is shrivelled.

Now the Latin:

Deformis quidem **a nemine**, quod sciam, qui modo me
vidit, sum unquam habitus. formosus **necne**, minus laboro:
statura fateo **non sum procera**... **sed neque exilis admo-
dum**... **nec ferrum tractare, nec stringere** quotidiano usu
exercitas **nescirem**;... Idem hodie animus, eadem vires,
oculi non idem; ita tamen extrinsecus **illaesi**, ita **sine
nube** clari ac lucidi, ut eorum qui acutissimum cernunt:
in hac solum parte, memet **invito**, simulator sum: in vultu,
quo '**nihil exsanguius** esse' dixit, is manet etiamnum color
exsangui & pallenti plane contrarius, ut quadragenario
major **vix sit cui non denis** prope annis, videar natura
minor: **neque corpore contracto neque cute.** (*CE* 8: 60)

Note first that in this small section of Latin prose there are
thirteen negative constructions. Four of these are already built
into the words themselves, **nescirem** (I did not know), **illaesi**
(undamaged), **invito** (involuntarily), **exsanguius** (more blood-
less), the original insult that provokes the defense, and its
rejection as **exsangui**... **contrarius**. Second, this passage has a
striking literary antecedent; both the use of **formosus** and the
negative construction derive from Virgil's second eclogue,
where Corydon, hopelessly in love with the **formosus pastor**,
reassures himself, having looked at his reflection in an un-
usually calm ocean, '**Nec sum adeo informis**... **si nunquam
fallit imago**'. But imagine the blind Milton, no longer able to see
himself in any mirror, calmly combining both **deformis** and
formosus in a single, defiant self-portrait (or perhaps we should
say ecphrasis), relying on the eyes of others for his mirror, the
eyes of others being what in the past he has claimed to shun.

But then the *Second Defense* turns to what *really* hurts: that
the *Regis Sanguinis Clamor* had been preceded with an epistle to
Charles II, comparing Milton to Polyphemus, not merely **deformis** but justly blinded by Odysseus: **monstrum horrendum,
informe . . . cui lumen ademptum**. Having defended his appearance, Milton writes:

> Would it were equally in my power to confute this un-
> human adversary on the subject of my blindness? But, it is
> not. Then, let us bear it. To be blind is not miserable; not to
> be able to bear blindness, that is miserable. But why should
> I be unable to bear that which it behoves every one to be
> prepared to bear, should the accident happen to himself,
> without repining? Why should I be unable to bear what I
> know may happen to any mortal being, what I know has
> actually happened to some of the most eminent and best of
> men, on the records of memory.   (*CE* 8: 63)

And he then proceeds to list not only Teresias and Phineus, the
precedents that survive into *Paradise Lost*, but also Timoleon of
Corinth, Appius Claudius, Caecilius Metellus, Dandolo, prince
of Venice, Ziske, 'the gallant duke of Bohemia', the humanist
Zanchius, and patriarch Isaac himself. I am less interested,
however, in the length and incoherence of this list in its first
form (we tend to think only of the version in *Paradise Lost*, 3:
33–36) than in the grammatical construction of the internal
consolation:

> Utinam de caecite pariter liceret **inhumanum** hunc
> refellere adversarium; **sed non licet**; feramus igitur:

non est miserum esse caecum; miserum est caecitatem non posse ferre. (*CE* 8: 63)

Beautifully simple, in its chiastic form, the defense of the blindness surpasses the defense of the appearance primarily in its full understanding of what negativity actually is: to be blind is not tragic; it is tragic not to be able to bear blindness. Out of this hard-won paradox, masquerading as textbook formula, Milton would fashion both the despair and the reconciliation of *Samson Agonistes*:

> O dark, dark, dark, amid the blaze of noon,
> Irrecoverably dark, total Eclipse
> Without all hope of day. (ll. 80–82)

> But he though blind of sight,
> Despis'd and thought extinguished quite,
> With inward eyes illuminated
> His fiery virtue rous'd
> From under ashes into sudden flame,
> And as an evening Dragon came. (ll. 1687–92)

In the *Second Defense*, Milton is not quite yet the evening Dragon. He still has to work out in laborious, confessional prose his testimony to the effect that his blindness is not a punishment for his defense of the regicides, but rather a sign of exceptional privilege:

> I am not conscious of any offense ... recently committed or long ago, the atrocity of which could have called down this calamity upon me above others ... I am still persuaded that I have written nothing, which was not right and true and pleasing to God. (*CE* 8: 67)

And here too the heart of the matter is conveyed in a negative syntax: **nullius ... nullius ... nihil non rectum ed vera**.

So we seem to have reached a point where Milton's negativity has found its true subject. It has gone beyond the modesty topos of being unseen, which is really, in the youthful poems, a boast, or the hortatory remarks to his father on not underestimating the value of a literary career, which we could put down to vocational hesitation, or the series of self-denying ordinances which mark the vocabulary, as well as the ethos, of *Comus*. Negativity has become the language of self-defense, which is the most purely negative form of self-promotion. As Milton scrutinizes all the recesses of his heart, and all his previous writings, none of them seems to him to have conceivably justified the wrath of an angry god. And the *Second Defense* continues for several pages to develop the thesis of heroic blindness brought about by his rigid adherence to duty.

> 'I neither repine at, nor repent me of my fate': **Me sortis meae neque pigere neque poenitere**; 'I neither believe, nor have found that God is angry': **Deam iratum neque sentire, neque habere.** 'The divine law, the divine favour, has made us not merely secure (**incolumes**), but, as it were, sacred from the injuries of men; nor would seem to have brought this darkness upon us so much by inducing a dimness of the eyes, as by the overshadowing of heavenly wings': **nec tam oculorum hebetudine, quam coelestium alarum umbra.** (*CE* 8: 72–73)

But why did Milton have to go through a negative syntax, an admission, as it were, of the adversary's position, in order to arrive at self-reassurance? In order to replace the ugly word **caecitas** with the glorious phrases **oculorum hebetudine** (which we might not unreasonably translate, remembering *Il Penseroso*, as 'a dim religious light') and **coelestium alarum umbra**, 'the shadow of angels' wings', he had, we might say, to look the worst in the face, to place it before our eyes, and his inward eyes, sentence after sentence, in order to deny its force, along with its grammatical and logical existence.

But we are still not finished. There is one more major encounter with Negation at the end of the *Second Defense*, after Milton has defended the leaders of the revolution, especially, of course, Oliver Cromwell. In this section of the tract, although the use of praise by negatives denied is not completely abandoned, it becomes merely a trace effect, completely overshadowed by the roll-call of real heroes, and the use of superlatives, which in Latin rise off the page like an alleluiah: **dignissimum, rectissimis, excellentissimo, fortissimorum**, and, piled into a single phrase, **modestissimos, & integerrimos, & fortissimos** (*CE* 8: 228). When promoting others, Milton did not hedge his grammatical bets. But he brought the *Defense* to a close, not with the defense of others, but again with defense of himself. Here is the final paragraph, in this case almost entirely in my own translation:

> As for myself, ... I have performed, certainly **not unwillingly**, I hope **not in vain**, the service which I thought would be most of use to the commonwealth ... If our last actions **should not sufficiently answer** the first, they themselves [the citizens] will see it. I have celebrated actions glorious, lofty, almost beyond praise, with testimony, I had almost

said a monument, which will **not speedily perish**; and if I **have done nothing else**, I have discharged my trust. As the epic poet . . . undertakes to embellish not the whole life of the hero whom he proposes to sing, but one particular action of his life . . . so likewise it should be enough either for my duty or for my excuse that I have celebrated at least one heroic action of my countrymen. If, after such brave things you are basely delinquent . . . posterity will speak and bring in the verdict: The foundation was strongly laid, the beginning and more than the beginning was famous; but it [posterity] will want to ask, **not without a certain mental disturbance**, who raised the entire work, who fastened the pediment? To such beginnings, such virtues, **if persever-ance was not added**, it will lament. It will see that the harvest of glory was abundant, but that **men did not match (defuisse)** the materials: but there **was not lacking (non defuisse)** one who could advise rightly, encourage, spur on, adorn both what was done and who did it, and could celebrate them with worthy praises for all ages to come.

What stands out in your mind as you read this? The certainty, or the doubt? The job has been done not unwillingly and not in vain, **haud gravatim** . . . **haud frustra** '*If* our last actions should not sufficiently answer . . . If I have done nothing else'. Milton is by now *more or less* confident that he has discharged the trust of which he spoke in the *Reason of Church Government*, although that was a covenant to leave behind a very different kind of monument. And why does he add that curious phrase, 'it should be enough either for my duty or for my **excuse**'? The Columbia edition translates, 'duty and excuse', but the Latin says firmly, **vel ad officium, vel ad excusationem**. Surely this prose leaves us, the readers, 'not without a certain mental disturbance', **non sine commotione quadam animi**; certainly not with 'calm of mind, all passion spent'.

It is a very good thing we do not have to leave the subject there. Because of course Milton did not have to rely on his defenses of the English republic for his monument to posterity. In his great poems, and especially in *Paradise Lost*, he added yet more complexity to the already complex structure of negative thought and expression.

As Kenneth Burke pointed out, 'the simplest route to negative theology is to make negatives of all terms that designate positive availability to sense perception (as *invisible, unknowable, boundless*).' Milton of course marshaled these and other such terms in his definition of God in the opening chapter of his *De Doctrina Christiana*. In Burke's secularized version of negative theology, 'such a description of *God* is also, necessarily, a statement about resources of language' (p. 457). But in *Paradise Lost* Milton was not translating negative theology into secular terms, he was critiquing it within a theological structure redesigned by himself. Orthodoxy of overall conviction grapples with heterodoxy of logical application, in the opening chapters of *De Doctrina* and to a lesser, or less clear, extent in *Paradise Lost*. As a sign of his orthodoxy he borrowed from Joshua Sylvester's translation of Du Bartas the theological version of the negative triplets he had discovered for use in the church-reform and divorce pamphlets. The Angelic song in Book 3 (l. 373) begins 'Thee Father ... | Immutable, Immortal, Infinite', words which form one great iambic pentameter. This was also the opening line of Sylvester's definition of God alone in the universe before Creation:

> God all in all, and all in God it was:
> Immutable, immortall, infinite,
> Incomprehensible, all spirit, all light,
> All Majestie, all-selfe-Omnipotent,
> Invisible, impassive, excellent.   (*First Day*, ll. 44–48)

But these are not the only positive negatives available to the sublime style. Milton used the strategy of the 'un-' to give his unique vision of an Edenic happiness into which, philosophically and theologically speaking, negativity had not yet penetrated:

> Our two first Parents, yet the only two
> Of mankind, in the happy Garden placed,
> Reaping immortal fruits of joy and love,
> **Uninterrupted** joy, **unrivall'd** love,
> In blissful solitude.   (*PL* 3: 65–68)

And in the same book (the most explicitly theological part of the poem), Milton used negative verbs to define his eccentric position on redemption, as expressed by the Son in defiance both of double predestination and Arminianism, of too little and too much human initiative:

> Father, thy word is passed, man shall find grace;
> And shall grace not find means, that finds her way,
> To speediest of thy winged messengers,

To visit all thy creatures, and to all
Comes unprevented, unimplor'd, unsought?   (*PL* 3: 227–31)

In this crucial triplet, the central term, 'unimplor'd', was Milton's coinage. It will be used again shortly.

But it turns out that some of the positive negatives of the poem are really negative after all. The fallen angels are, Satan says, 'irreconcilable to our grand Foe' (*PL* 1: 122), their 'mind and spirit remains | invincible' (1: 141), their strength 'undiminished' (1: 154). These half-praises compete with the negatives of self pity. In 'inextinguishable fire' (2: 88), they must remain 'unrespited, unpitied, unreprieved' (2: 185). Yet exactly the same formula—the three un-words that make up one strong pentameter line—is used for genuine praise. Against the would-be undoing force of the fallen angels' despair, the poem posits the idea of steadfastness, in the definition of the angel Abdiel's position during the rebellion,

> Among innumerable false, unmoved,
> Unshaken, unseduced, unterrified.   (5: 897–98)

This, as we will see, foreshadows *lexically* the courage of Jesus in *Paradise Regained*. There is a struggle going on, it appears, between negative constructions that have been corralled by the false heroism, the old epic values, of the fallen angels, and those that anticipate the new heroism of passive resistance.

As with theology, so also with poetics; *Lycidas* had challenged Milton to make sure that Edward King was not 'unwept', but now Milton produces a cluster of words which speak to his much larger poetic ambition. In the invocation to Book 1 he claims that *this* poem will reach for 'Things unattempted yet in prose or rhyme', a more resonant statement than Ariosto's *cosa non detta in prosa mai, ne in rime*, to which, of course, it replies by upstaging. In the invocation to Book 3 he appeals to the principle of Light that he may 'express thee unblamed', a new twist to the notion of 'unreproved' that in *L'Allegro* so lightly invoked the realm of the thou-shalt-not. In the invocation to Book 7 he warns that 'Half yet remains unsung', a word that gathers propositional as well as structural force in the invocation to Book 9, where he deplores the captivity of previous epics to military values, 'the better fortitude | Of Patience and Heroic Martyrdom | Unsung'. And let's not forget, in this cluster, the famously disingenuous statement that his verse is 'unpremeditated' (9: 24), and that he himself, like Abdiel, is in the defeat of the Restoration 'unchang'd | To hoarse or mute, though fall'n on evil days' (7: 24–25). Perhaps more poignantly still, in the invocation to Book 9 he claims that his celestial muse visits him 'unimplor'd' (l. 22), thus echoing his coinage defining the free gift of grace to humans. The cluster of these terms—let us call them the terms of the poetic mandate to do what has not been done before and might still be dangerous—in the poem's four invocations is far from accidental.

Given the vocational importance of 'unsung' in Milton's vocabulary (and it will return significantly at the opening of *Paradise Regained*), it is rather startling to find that Astarte, one of the most important of the pagan deities listed in Book 1, is described as 'not unsung' in Sion (*PL* 1: 442)—that is to say, her worship has spread from Syria into Israel. And by similar token we should notice that Satan enters Paradise 'all unobserved, unseen' (4: 130), a formula Milton had adopted to describe his 'own' relation to the world in *Il Penseroso* and *L'Allegro*. Does this leakage of a special, privileged, positive negativity into the territory of the demonic mean that the negative formulation is not so significant as we thought it was, merely, after all, a lexical, Latinate habit? Or should we thereby recognize Satan as a demonic blend of L'Allegro, Il Penseroso, and the poet himself? *L'Allegro* ends by calling its catalog of the pleasures of the eye 'these delights'. Something has happened to the aesthetic sense (blindness, perhaps), when landing in Paradise 'the Fiend | Saw undelighted all delight', a phrase which is not merely a negative, not merely an oxymoron, but also Milton's coinage, borrowed from the *Doctrine and Discipline of Divorce*.

I want to argue that Milton is not just using his philological reflexes at such moments, but demanding that we pay attention to what is truly a negative, truly a positive, though the mere grammatical form of words and sentences may at first glance obscure that extraordinarily difficult distinction, never more difficult than in a poem where the Adversary has declared 'Evil be thou my good', and tempted so many of Milton's readers into some version of skepticism or Manicheism. The distinction becomes more difficult to make when the negative and positive electrodes are built into the word itself, and into an already complex word, as is characteristic of *Paradise Lost*, rather than being the result of a relatively simple 'not' formula, as in the anxious autobiographical passages in the prose.

How far can Milton stretch this exercise, and our minds? Almost to the point of humor. In Book 6, during the War in Heaven, Satan exercises extreme ingenuity in the verbal as well as the chemical sphere. Having arranged for the discovery of gunpowder and its processing into military explosives, he has the nerve to tell his legions that what they need is 'not uninvented' (6: 470). This is only the first, if the wittiest, of a series of double negatives that recall the puzzling 'not unseen' of *L'Allegro*, and also require some thought, as in 'something not unseasonable to ask' (8: 210). Eve, let us note, was not 'uninformed | Of...marriage rites' (a coinage first used in *Martin Bucer* of Milton himself, but here applied to the prior training or sexual instinct one might want in a wife), and imagines that the fruit might make her intellectually superior to Adam, 'a thing not undesirable' (9: 824), which causes us to ask, 'not undesirable to whom?' Sin's proposal, on the other hand, that it is 'Not unagreeable' to build a bridge between Hell and Earth (10: 256), causes us to ask 'not unagreeable' to whom with a darker irony. The larger other project of Sin and Death is to 'destroy, and unimmortal make | All kinds' (10: 611–12), which is equally perverse, and Milton's coinage to boot; as though language had to stretch to encompass the eschatological narrative perhaps too simply and conventionally stated in the very second line of the poem, where we are invited to hear how 'mortal taste | Brought Death into the World'. Yet another Miltonic coinage generated by these dark powers is 'unhidebound', a description of Death on his way out of Hell and anticipating a feast of humans (10: 601), which has puzzled Milton's editors, since it seems to contradict *itself*.

There are literally dozens of other instances, though few as striking as these. A proper stylistician would count all the instances in *Paradise Lost*, and draw statistical conclusions about Milton's negativity, here and elsewhere. I believe, however, that even this mode of selective quotation shows how much deeper and richer Milton's grasp of the negative had become by 1667, so that what was merely a lexical habit, however underwritten by experience, now reveals itself as language's daring search for the previously inconceivable.

I cannot, however, ignore *Paradise Regained* and *Samson Agonistes*. In these two poems, it seems to me, Milton's negativity resolves itself into two different and simpler patterns from what we have partially followed in *Paradise Lost*, which may reflect on the stages of their composition. In *Samson Agonistes*, there is both a proportional decrease in the number of negative constructions and a tendency for the complex word that takes negative form to simply carry a negative meaning. First there is the negativity of blindness, 'irrecoverably dark' (l. 81) and 'inseparably dark' (l. 154). Then there is his regret for his 'former servitude' to Dalila, 'ignoble | Unmanly, ignominious, infamous' (ll. 416–17). Then Manoa advises Samson no longer to serve the Philistines with his miraculous strength. 'Better at home lie bedrid, not only idle, | Inglorious, unemploy'd' (ll. 579–80). Samson complains of 'maladies innumerable' (l. 608) and of 'wounds immedicable' (l. 620), a word Milton learned to use in *Colasterion* (*CPW* 2: 737), and which reminds us that this poem, if finished late, is uncomfortably close to the divorce pamphlets in feeling. Dalila begs Samson not to be strong primarily in 'uncompassionate anger' (l. 181), and Samson replies that her behavior to him has raised in him 'inexpiable hate' (l. 839). These melancholy constructions are more powerful, I suggest, especially as they accumulate, than the opening, conventionally heroic adjectives that describe Samson as he once was, 'Irresistible Samson' (l. 126),

or the 'invincible might' (l. 1271) that the Chorus hope God will
once again put into the hands of his deliverer, all adjectives that
remind us of the defiant fallen angels, and ask precisely the
questions about Milton's view of violence that recent events
have brought back into the foreground of Milton criticism. But
I do not see in *Samson Agonistes* any of the truly philosophical
conundrums, the no-yes-no and perhaps yes again constructions
which mark the mature style of *Paradise Lost*.

On the other hand, in *Paradise Regained* Milton seems to go
out of his way to recover the youthful, innocent, and Stoic force
of the simpler negative marked by un-. For in this poem we are
assured that humility—not thrusting oneself forward—is
essential to modern heroism, or to modern ideas of heroism.
Thus the opening lines of the poem express a series of para-
doxes:

> Thou Spirit who led'st this glorious Eremite
> Into the Desert, his Victorious Field
> Against the Spiritual Foe, and brought'st him thence
> By proof th'undoubted Son of God, inspire,
> As thou are wont, my prompted Song, else mute,
>
>   .   .   .   .
>   ... to tell of deeds
> Above Heroic, though in secret done,
> And unrecorded left through many an Age,
> Worthy t'have not remain'd so long unsung.   (*PR* 1: 8–17)

The protagonist of this poem is, like that of *Il Penseroso*,
'obscure, | unmarkt, unknown' (1: 24–25) when he comes to
his coming-out occasion, the baptism by St. John. And at the

end of the poem, of course, 'Hee unobserv'd | Home to his Mother's house private return'd'. I say 'of course' because the demureness of Jesus' victory over temptation, and his ethos of delay and renunciation, have been understood by everyone who reads the poem. What *has* been unmarked and unknown is the way the vocabulary of this ethos maps onto and is quietly empowered by the long stream of Milton's negative constructions heretofore, constructions which began, apparently, when he contemplated the problems of his own tardiness and invisibility in the field he hoped would make him famous.

In the person of Jesus, before he begins his ministry, Milton was able to solve the psychological and ethical problems of reputation and of fame. At last he can demonstrate what 'passive fortitude' must really mean, which *Paradise Lost*, still in urgent communication with classical epic, was unable to do. There is now a *structural* relationship between being 'unsung' and 'unknown' and the particular kind of heroism Jesus manages, which comes from doing nothing. He feels no fear and he doubts no doubts, 'unshaken' and 'unappall'd' and having an 'untroubl'd mind' even after Satan's more active, physical threats in Book 4. He is 'invincible' (*PR* 2: 408) only in his temperance, thus canceling out the militarist use of that word both in *Paradise Regained* and its nostalgic echo in *Samson Agonistes*. Accordingly, the diminished Satan in this poem is not allowed to garner the power of the great extremist negatives marshaled in Satan's speeches in *Paradise Lost*, Book 1. The only ones he is still allowed are the smaller, elegiac ones, 'unfortunate' (1: 358) and 'unpitied' (1: 414), or the brilliant Miltonic coinage, 'unconniving', used by nobody else subsequently, a word which Satan had to invent to obscure the question of whether his freedom to exit from Hell now and then was really by divine permission or his own enterprise:

> Yet to that hideous place *not* so confined
> By rigor unconniving but that oft
> Leaving my dolorous Prison I enjoy
> Large liberty.   (1: 362–65)

This is glossed by Hughes as 'unwinking', ever watchful, a gloss that obscures the theological issue as how much of Satan's activity on earth God is responsible for. In fact, the word 'connive' more often carried already, in Milton's day, its modern meaning or meanings, of which the most usual is 'to shut one's eyes to an action that one ought to oppose, but which one covertly sympathizes with; to wink *at*, be secretly privy or accessory to'. And surely Milton was here echoing, with a peculiarly ironic inflection, the particularly nasty speech of God in *Paradise Lost*, in which he enjoys watching Satan, Sin, and Death 'impute | Folly to me... that with so much ease'

> I suffer them to enter and possess
> A place so heav'nly, and *conniving* seem
> To gratify my scornful Enemies.   (10: 623–25)

Moreover, Satan explicitly renounces the *good* Stoic negatives that characterize the Son. 'The wisest, unexperienc't', he warns, 'will be ever | Timorous and loth, with novice modesty... | Irresolute, unhardy, unadvent'rous' (*PR* 3: 240–43). This is a version of the voice in Milton's own ear that he imagined in the *Reason of Church Government* berating him for his inactivity in behalf of church reform, and Milton's response had been to enter the fray. But novice modesty in *Paradise Regained* is to be a lasting condition of the mind. 'Prediction else', the Son responds to the temptation of the kingdoms, 'Will unpredict' (4: 395), a mind-defying paradox, both theological and philosophical, of which Milton is the first inventor and the one and only user.

Perhaps

To predict is to express confidence in one's knowledge of the future. To unpredict is to express disappointment, disillusionment, or perhaps, if it is someone else's prediction that has failed, *Schadenfreude*. If one is not absolutely confident about futurity, one may wish to employ the word **perhaps**. **Perhaps** has an old native root, 'hap', which Milton actually uses to express Satan's luck in finding Eve alone (*PL* 9: 421). It is a perhaps a better concept with which to end this book than with Milton's complex negativity, even when it is the negative expression of the possible, as in 'it is not impossible', a famous locution from *Areopagitica*. 'Yet is it not impossible that [Truth] may have more shapes than one.' **Perhaps** seems a much smaller word, and at first less Miltonic. Milton was not often tentative, and when in argument tended to use locutions like this: 'No man who knows ought, can be so stupid to deny that...' from the *Tenure of Kings and Magistrates* (*CPW* 3: 198). Even in the *Tenure*, however, he hoped that the Long Parliament might '**perhaps** in future ages, if they prove not too degenerate,...look up with honour, and aspire toward these exemplary and matchless deeds of thir Ancestors' (3: 237). 'Perhaps' is perhaps worthy not to have been so long unconsidered.

The dictionaries tell us that **perhaps** is an adverb, though as Milton uses it is often difficult to discover what verb it modifies. At times it seems to acquire a prophetic force of its own. It also happens to be a word that Milton associated with his own writerly ambitions. In his first significant usage of the word, he placed it in a prominently narcissistic position in Sonnet 7, in relation to his 'twenty-third year', a date that forced him to confront his lack of poetic productivity thus far: '**Perhaps** my semblance might deceive the truth | That I to manhood am arriv'd so near.' At the end of *Of Reformation* he casts himself in the role of the new bard: 'Then amidst the Hymns and Halle-luiahs of Saints some one may **perhaps** be heard offering at high strains in new and lofty Measures to sing and celebrate thy divine Mercies' (*CPW* 1: 616). In *Animadversions* he suggests that 'he that now for haste snatches up a plain ungarnisht present as a thanke-offering to thee, ... May then **perhaps** take up a Harp, and sing thee an elaborate Song to Generations (*CPW* 1: 706). In the *Reason of Church Government* he describes how the admiration of his friends abroad helped him to believe that 'I might **perhaps** leave something so written to aftertimes, as they should not willingly let it die' (*CPW* 1: 810). The word is used twice more in the same autobiographical section of the tract, the second time to express a certain diffidence: 'Time serves not now, and **perhaps I might seem too profuse to give any certain account of what the mind ... hath liberty to propose to herself**' (1: 812–13). There are several more appear-ances in the *Apology*, all in the general context of how one should write controversy, the last being also in the apocalyptic or prophetic mode of *Of Reformation*: 'he that looks well into

the book of Gods Providence, if he read there that God for this
their negligence and halting, brought all that following persecution upon this Church, and on themselves, **perhaps** will be
found at the last day not to have read amisse' (1: 943).

This pattern is simply too strong to see as casual, especially
when **perhaps** is nowhere used in a neutral or casual way in the
church reform pamphlets. But look what happens in the *Doctrine and Discipline of Divorce*, when Milton is staking out his
own qualifications for raising the issue. 'But', he asks rhetoric-
ally, 'this question concerns not us **perhaps**'. And he ends his
preface with two demurrals: The tract might '**perhaps** more fitly
have bin writt'n in another tongue', Latin of course; and '**perhaps also heer I might have ended nameless**' (*CPW* 2: 233).

In *Areopagitica* Milton uses our little word 7 times. Of these,
no less than 4 are marshaled when he turns, in heat, to describing
what is evidently his own experience with the practical difficulties and humiliations of the licensing system. The passage is
essential to our understanding of Milton's understanding of
his own turn to political pamphleteering, and deserves quotation
at some length, not least because it seems to cancel Sonnet 7:

> When a man writes to the world, he summons up all his
> reason and deliberation to assist him; he searches, med-
> itats, is industrious, and likely consults and confers with
> his judicious friends; . . . if in this the most consummate
> act of his fidelity and ripenesse, no years, no industry, no
> former proof of his abilities can bring him to that state of
> maturity, as not to be still mistrusted and suspected,
> unless he carry all his considerat diligence, all his mid-

night watchings, and expence of Palladian oyl, to the
hasty view of an unleasur'd licencer, **perhaps** much his
younger, **perhaps** far his inferiour in judgement, **perhaps** one who never knew the labour of book-writing,
and if he be not repulst, or slighted, must appear in Print
like a punie with his guardian, and his censors hand on
the back of his title, to be his bayl and surety…And
what if the author shall be one so copious of fancie, as to
have many things well worth the adding, come into his
mind after licencing, while the book is yet under the
Presse, which not seldom happ'ns to the best and diligent-
est writers; and that **perhaps** a dozen times in one book.
The Printer dares not go beyond his licenc'd copy; so often
then must the author trudge to his leav-giver, that thos his
new insertions may be view'd.   (*CPW* 2: 532)

Although Milton does not here use the 'he who' form of indirec-
tion, it is clear that the 'man' in question is a portrait of himself in
1644, now confident of his 'ripenesse' (at the age of 36), and rather
prickly on the subject of how hard it is to write a book. His quarrel
with licensing is both downright practical and highly principled,
and it is the same 'man' who will reappear a few pages later as
the chivalric protagonist in the 'wars of Truth' (2: 562). And this,
not coincidentally, is where **perhaps** herself reappears in a semi-
allegorical context, very different from the book trade:

For who knows not [one of Milton's lexical confidence
tricks, of which *Areopagitica* has dozens] that Truth is
strong next to the Almighty;…give her but room, & do
not bind her when she sleeps, for then she speaks not

true, as the old Proteus did, who spake oracles only when
he was caught & bound, but then rather she turns herself
into all shapes, except her own, and **perhaps** tunes her
voice according to the time.   (*CPW* 2: 562–63)

The brilliance of the final perception, which Milton owed to
Bacon's aphorism, 'authoriz'd books are but the language of the
times', is actually increased by the subtle placement of **perhaps**,
which insists that we give it ontological weight. Think of it as a
joint between the present and the future.

I want to suggest that this lexical habit, of giving more content
to this little word of doubt than we normally expect, was carried
over into *Paradise Lost*, where past, present, and future meet.
This continues my argument that Milton learned how to write in
the world of prose polemic, and that when he abandoned its
causes he kept some of its tools. One of the most important lines
in *Paradise Lost*, itself a description of something very small and
often overlooked, tells of the creation of the ant:

> First crept
> The Parsimonious Emmet, provident
> Of Future, in small room large heart enclos'd
> Pattern of just equality **perhaps**
> Hereafter, join'd in her popular Tribes
> Of Commonalty: (7: 484–89)

The small word sits in the middle of a subtle train of alliter-
ations (parsimonious, provident, pattern, perhaps, popular); it
is notoriously difficult to decide whether it looks backward or
forward syntactically, not least because there is no verb for it to

modify. Does its ability to doubt apply best to 'pattern' or to 'just equality' or to 'Hereafter', or all three? This is one of the features of Milton's fluid and surprising syntax that Christopher Ricks identified as providing charm, especially used in relation to Eve (*Milton's Grand Style*, 89–95). But here we have something considerably more interesting than charm. We have a hesitant political prophecy. And it is all the more important for echoing some sentences in the prose works. Consider *A Treatise of Civil Power in Ecclesiastical Causes*, whose opening address slightly delays identifying the target audience: 'To them who **perhaps hereafter**, less experienc'd in religion, may come to govern or give us laws, this or other such, if they please, may be a timely instruction' (*CPW* 7: 241). Or, more directly related, the passage added for the second edition of *Readie & Easie Way*:

> they who think the nation undon without a king, . . . have
> not so much true spirit and understanding in them as a
> pismire: neither are these diligent creatures hence con-
> cluded to live in lawless anarchie or that commended, but
> are set the examples to imprudent and ungoverned men,
> of a frugal and self-governing democratie or Common-
> wealth: safer and more thriving in the joint providence
> and counsel of many industrious equals, then under the
> single domination of one imperious Lord.   (7: 427)

By the time he wrote *Paradise Lost* Milton had abandoned the hope that the English would follow this example of a polity except **perhaps hereafter**; but its very relinquishment to the territory of doubt gives value back to the idea, a 'large heart' enclosed in a small emblem. He even allows back into the formula the word 'popular' that had given him so much trouble in *REW*.

To conclude, I shall cite three other instances from *Paradise Lost*, where readers may see for themselves how extraordinarily complex are the tasks to which Milton has learned to apply **perhaps**. They share the dignity of drawing attention to three of the poem's greatest subjects: the expansion of cosmic knowledge; our ignorance of what it means to die; and the ontological status of the two great sexes. First, there is the cunning simile describing Satan's brief landing on the surface of the sun:

> There lands the Fiend, a spot like which **perhaps**
> Astronomer in the Sun's lucent Orb
> Through his glaz'd OpticTube yet never saw.   (3: 588–90)

Technically, as an adverb, 'perhaps' governs 'saw'; but can you tell me where its uncertainty actually lands, on the existence of Galileo, or on his discovery of sunspots which admit flaws in heaven, or on Satan's resemblance to a sunspot in ontological terms, or on 'yet' and 'never', which have no normal business with each other, and which throw the whole comparison into disarray?

Next comes Satan's most ingenious rhetorical move when persuading Eve not to take seriously (that is to say, literally) the dreadful warning that eating the forbidden fruit will result in death, a trick enabled by her ignorance of the content of the word 'death':

> So ye shall die **perhaps**, by putting off
> Human, to put on Gods, death to be wisht.   (9: 713–14)

And, as a direct consequence of the success of this move, Eve considers keeping the effects of the Tree of Knowledge to herself:

> But to Adam in what sort
> Shall I appear? Shall I to him make known
> As yet my change, and give him to partake
> Full happiness with mee, or rather not.
> But keep the odds of Knowledge in my power
> Without Copartner? So to add what wants
> In Female Sex, the more to draw his Love,
> And render me more equal, and **perhaps**,
> A thing not undesirable, sometime
> Superior.   (9: 816–25)

In this last and (from Milton) unexpected ploy, 'perhaps' should govern, retroactively, 'render me', but in fact it pulls forward to the end of the sentence, to hesitate between 'a thing not undesirable' and 'sometime superior'. But is it 'sometime' in the future, or 'some times' in the relationship? If we remember that moment of political prophecy symbolized by the ant, 'emblem of just equality **perhaps** hereafter' and if we are prepared to read *Paradise Lost* as an apology for the divorce pamphlets, 'sometime' meets 'hereafter' in the territory of gender generosity, and 'more equal' (an oxymoron, surely) meets 'just equality' in a world where words can make things better.

PERTINENT READING

Milton Criticism

Achinstein, Sharon. *Milton and the Revolutionary Reader*. Princeton, 1994. [A rich discussion of linguistic contexts of the revolutionary era.]

Anselment, Raymond. *'Betwixt Jest and Earnest': Marprelate, Milton, Marvell, Swift and the decorum of religious ridicule*. Toronto, 1979.

Burke, Edmund. *A Philosophical Enquiry into the origin of our ideas of the sublime and beautiful*, Section 4, 'The effect of words' (1757).

Burke, Kenneth. *Language as Symbolic Action*. Berkeley and Los Angeles, 1968.

Clark, Donald L. *John Milton at St. Paul's School: A Study of Ancient Rhetoric in English Renaissance Education*. New York, 1948.

Corns, Thomas. *The Development of Milton's Prose Style*. Oxford, 1982.

—— *Milton's Language*. Oxford, 1990.

Diekhoff, John S. *Milton on Himself. Milton's Utterances upon Himself and his Works*. London, 1939.

Edwards, Karen, 'Milton's Reformed Animals: An Early Modern Bestiary', *Milton Quarterly*, 39:4 (2005).

Eliot, T. S. *On Poetry and Poets*. New York, 1961. Contains 'Milton I', previously published as 'A Note on the Verse of John Milton', *Essays and Studies* 21 (1936), and 'Milton II', a revised version of the British Academy lecture (1947).

Fallon, Stephen. 'Alexander More Reads Milton: Self-Representation and Anxiety in Milton's *Defences*', in Graham Parry and Joan Raymond (eds.), *Milton and the Terms of Liberty*. Cambridge, 2002.

Fish, Stanley. *How Milton Works*. Cambridge, Mass., 2001. [Esp. Chs. 10 and 11, on *Paradise Regained*.]

Fletcher, Harris F. *John Milton's Intellectual Development*, 2 vols. Urbana, Ill., 1956–61.

Hale, John K. *Milton's Languages*. Cambridge, 1997.

—— 'Milton and the Rationale of Insulting', in Stephen Dobranski and John Rumrich (eds.), *Milton and Heresy*. Cambridge, 1998. [A spirited defense of Milton's rude words.]

Haskin, Dayton. *Milton's Burden of Interpretation*. Philadelphia, 1994. [Ch. 6, on *Paradise Regained*.]

Jeffko, Walter. 'Redefining Death', in Edwin Schneidman (ed.), *Death: Current Perspectives*. Palo Alto, Calif., 1976, rev. 1980.

Kahn, Victoria. 'Allegory and the Sublime in *Paradise Lost*', in Annabel Patterson (ed.), *John Milton*. Harlow, 1992, 192–96.

—— 'The Metaphorical Contract in Milton's *Tenure of Kings and Magistrates*', in David Armitage, Armand Himy, and Quentin Skinner (eds.), *Milton and Republicanism*. Cambridge, 1995.

Kastenberg, Robert, and Ruth Aisenberg, 'The Psychology of Death', in Edwin Schneidman (ed.), *Death: Current Perspectives*. Palo Alto, Calif., 1976, rev. 1980.

Kerrigan, William. *The Prophetic Milton*. Charlottesville, 1974. [Esp. Ch. 3, on 'our', 'see/saw', 'now', and double negatives.]

Kranidas, Thomas. *Milton and the Rhetoric of Zeal*. Pittsburgh, 2005.

Leavis, F. R. 'Milton's Verse', in *Revaluation*. New York, 1947, 1963.

Le Comte, Edward, *Milton and Sex*. London, 1978.

Lewalski, Barbara. *Milton's Brief Epic: The Genre, Meaning, and Art of 'Paradise Regained'*. London, 1966.

Lieb, Michael. 'Milton's *Of Reformation* and the Dynamics of Controversy', in Michael Lieb and John T. Shawcross (eds.), *Achievements of the Left Hand: Essays on the Prose of John Milton*. Amherst, 1974.

Loewenstein, David, and James Grantham Turner (eds.). *Politics, Poetics, and Hermeneutics in Milton's Prose*. Cambridge, 1990. [Esp. essay by Knoppers on *Readie & Easie Way*.]

Mohl, Ruth. *John Milton and his Commonplace Book*. New York, 1969.

Neumann, Joshua H. 'Milton's Prose Vocabulary', *PMLA* 60 (1945), 102–20.

Norbrook, David. *Writing the English Republic: Poetry, Rhetoric, and Politics, 1627–1660*. Cambridge, 1999. [Esp. Ch. 10, on Satan's republican language.]

Ramachandran, Ayesha, 'Worldmaking in Early Modern Europe: Global Imaginations from Montaigne to Milton', Ph.D. diss., Yale University, 2008.

Raymond, Joad. 'The King is a Thing', in Graham Parry and Joad Raymond (eds.), *Milton and the Terms of Liberty*. Cambridge, 2002.

Ricks, Christopher. *Milton's Grand Style*. Oxford, 1963.

Rogers, John, 'Milton and the Heretical Priesthood of Christ', in David Loewenstein and John Marshall (eds.), *Heresy, Literature and Politics in Early Modern English Culture*. Cambridge, 2006.

Sanchez, Reuben. 'From Polemic to Prophecy: Milton's Uses of Jeremiah in *The Reason of Church Government* and 'The Readie and Easie Way', *Milton Studies*, 30 (1993), 27–44.

Shawcross, John. 'The Chronology of Milton's Major Poems', *PMLA* 76 (1961), 345–58.

Shuger, Deborah. *Sacred Rhetoric: The Christian Grand Style in the English Renaissance*. Princeton, 1988.

Stavely, Keith. *The Politics of Milton's Prose Style*. New Haven, 1975.

Stein, Arnold, 'Imagining Death: The Ways of Milton', *Milton Studies*, 29 (1993), pp. 107–18.

Stewart, Stanley. 'Milton revises *The Readie and Easie Way*', *Milton Studies*, 20 (1984), 205–24.

Turner, James Grantham, *One Flesh: Paradisal Marriage and Sexual Relations in the Age of Milton*. Oxford, 1987.

Webber, Joan. *The Eloquent I: Style and Self in Seventeenth-Century Prose*. Madison, Wis., 1968.

Williams, Raymond. *Keywords: A Vocabulary of Culture and Society*. Oxford, 1976, rev. 1983.

Worden, Blair. *Literature and Politics in Cromwellian England*. Oxford, 2007.

Tools and Resources

Darbishire, Helen (ed.). *The Early Lives of Milton*. London, 1932.

Happe, Peter, *The Complete Plays of John Bale*, 2 vols. Boydell, 1986.

Ingram, William and Kathleen Swaim, *Concordance to Milton's English Poetry*. Oxford, 1972.

Lewalski, Barbara, *The Life of John Milton: A Critical Biography*. Oxford, 2000.

Parker, William Riley. *Milton: A Biography*, 2 vols. Oxford, 1968, rev. Gordon Campbell, 1996.

Patterson, F. A. et al. (eds.). *The Works of John Milton*, 18 vols. in 21, New York, 1931–8. [Columbia Edition]

Sterne, Laurence, and Harold Kollmeier (eds.). *Concordance to the English Prose of John Milton*. Binghamton, NY, 1985.

Wolfe, Don M. et al. (eds.). *Complete Prose Works of John Milton*, 8 vols. New Haven, 1953–82.

INDEX